Meeting at the Well

A JEWISH SPIRITUAL GUIDE TO BEING ENGAGED

Daniel Judson
and Nancy H. Wiener

With a Foreword by Rabbi Lawrence A. Hoffman, Ph.D.

UAHC Press • New York, New York

For Sandy
You are my fountain in the garden,
my well of living waters
that stream from Lebanon.
DAN

For Judy
You have taught me the art
of communication
and enabled me to grow
in immeasurable ways.
NANCY

Library of Congress Cataloging-in-Publication Data

Judson, Dan.
　Meeting at the well : a Jewish spiritual guide to engagement /
　Dan Judson and Nancy Wiener.
　　p. cm.
　ISBN 0-8074-0753-4 (pbk. : alk. paper)
　1. Betrothal—Religious apsects—Judaism. 2. Betrothal—
　United States. 3. Jewish way of life.
　I. Wiener, Nancy H., 1958–　II. Title

　BM713.J83 2002
　296.7'4—dc21　　　　　　　　　　　　　2002020187

Acknowledgments

The idea for this book was solely and completely Dr. Sandy Falk's, who is the source of all of Dan's good ideas. Dr. Kerry Olitzky provided initial encouragement, and Rabbi Josh and Leah Caruso provided initial inspiration. Francie Levine-Grater, Nancy Judson, and Dr. Lydia Bernstein all edited early versions of this work.

We would like to thank Rabbi Hara Person at the UAHC Press for her excitement about the project and her dedication in shepherding this book through the publication process. Lynn Levy at the UAHC provided important insights as we prepared the manuscript. Thanks are due to all those at the UAHC Press who each contributed their skills to this book: Ken Gesser, Stuart Benick, Rick Abrams, Liane Broido, Debra Hirsch Corman, Rachel Gleiberman, and Benjamin David. We also thank the CCAR for permission to reprint the statement on Reform Jewish Sexual Values.

We would like to thank the following people for their invaluable contributions: David and Vera Beinstein, John Beuker, Anne Berlin and Sara Winthrop, Drs. Shai and Rebecca Cherry, Martha Hausman, Rabbi Neil Kominsky, Jessica Kurtz, Rabbi Aaron Lever, Dinah McNamara, Rabbi Michelle Missaghieh and Bruce Ellman, Rabbis David and Jennie Rosenn, Rabbi Keith Stearn, Craig and Lori Sumberg, and Nadine Vantine-Kelley.

Contents

Foreword

Weddings matter supremely—not just in North America, but universally. That is saying something. Given all the diversity of the thousands of societies that anthropologists have studied, there is not much that cuts so clearly across time, space, and culture. Births do not; in many places, birth is marked by no ritual whatsoever. It is true that death never goes unnoticed—how could it?—but burials can be tiny private affairs, "private funerals," as they are known today. Weddings, too, need not be lavish formal ceremonies. People do elope, after all, and throughout time, people have chosen to live together until, eventually, they were seen ex post facto as the permanent couple they are. But by and large, every culture we know prefers to ritualize weddings, to publicize them as important communal events—which, in fact, is what they are.

The actual couple being married may not expect all this public coverage. They may think of their marriage as personal, intimate, irrelevant to the world outside themselves. But, in fact, there is a reason for this cultural accent on weddings. Historically speaking, weddings have little to do with romantic love, and much to do with extending family bonds. In preindustrialist societies, weddings constituted useful alliances. And even today, parents recognize that the person their son or daughter marries comes with "their" own family who will now be included in celebrations and be consulted about personal problems and plans. Ritualist Ronald Grimes comments, "Couples insist that this event is 'their wedding,' yet many customs make it all too evident that the occasion belongs as much to their families as to themselves." Romanticism aside, marriage (it turns out) is about whole families.

But still, even marriages that are for families do not happen without couples, and here is where engagement comes in. Unlike the wedding, which involves "everyone," engagement is that fabulous, totally unparalleled, and absolutely unique opportunity for the couple alone to figure out who they are and what they will be, together.

Engagements are very old. Romans had them; so too did Jews in the Greco-Roman world. But engagement, as we know it today, is also very new—altogether different in an era when couples have already become their own entity, are probably living together, and in any event, are contemplating marriage not as members of families but as themselves, divinely gifted individuals with hopes of committing themselves to a relationship that will enhance each other's happiness and blessing. Unlike the wedding, which remains the joint possession of the couple and their families, engagement is the couple's opportune time to own and to enjoy. The problem is that so many couples fail to take advantage of it. Hence this book: a sensitive guide to couples of all sorts as they chart their way through "engagementhood."

For most people, engagement is just something that happens in between being single and being married. Happen it will. But the point of this book is that it need not happen inconsequentially. In its own way, it is as important as the marriage period that follows. It occurs at the same time as wedding plans are being made. But it is not at all the same thing. Confusing engagement with planning for a wedding is a terrible error, aided and abetted by wedding magazines that miss altogether the importance of the engagement moment. Modern weddings pose as events for couples, but as anyone who has planned one knows, they are equally about two families joining as one. They evoke anxieties on all sides. Wedding conversations are about whom to choose as flower girl (and whom to leave out!), how many (from our side) we can invite, whom the "other family" will bring, and how we negotiate social space and time with someone else's family that is (at the same time) about to become our own.

An engagement, however, is potentially precious to no one but the couple about to marry. Subtract the wedding plans, and engagement remains alone, as what it uniquely is: a period betwixt and between—no longer single but not yet married, gifted with a space in time to contemplate the fullness of what togetherness might mean.

This betwixt and between period is technically called "liminal," from the Latin word for a doorframe, limen. Picture yourself walking from an anteroom with cocktails into a sit-down dinner, where, however, no one has provided a seating plan. You stop in the doorway to wonder where you will sit. Or imagine walking through an entryway to a school carnival or job fair. You stop at the door to decide where to go. Doorways are stopping places; they demand you think your next step through. You cannot linger there forever—someone will complain eventually, "Excuse me, aren't you moving inside?" So too with engagement. You cannot stay there endlessly; the whole point is to look forward to the room of life called marriage: new home, new name (maybe), new social entity (certainly). "I am my beloved's; my beloved is mine," says Song of Songs. That is the new room that beckons. But in the meantime, how do you take advantage of the limen, the doorway to your future?

Anthropologist Victor Turner has said that liminal periods provide ideal opportunities to plan creatively. God knows, that is what couples about to be married need most-both planning and creativeness. Planning is obvious: Where will we live? How will we get along when you and I have to work at different jobs with different stresses? What do we do with old friends who are either "mine" or "yours," but not "ours"? Who does the cooking? How do we handle money? How will we show our love?

Less appreciated is the word "creatively." People enter adulthood already formed by lifetime habits of thought. But now they meet that special "other," and they have two choices: to persist unthinkingly in old ways of thought or to open up options to creative growth together. A woman I know has always been a victim; she was abused as a child. Now she is getting married. How does she properly retain that real memory but construct a new life with her husband, who really loves her? Then there is the man who loves to spend time alone with his coin collection. Fair enough. But how does he moderate his passion for solitude, given his wife-to-be's desire for an active social life? I choose these cases only as examples of the creative working through of lifestyles that successful marriage demands and engagement offers. We all have hopes. Marriage can mean hopes multiplied exponentially—but only if the partners take the effort to hope together.

Now we see why this is a book to recommend to every engaged couple. Wedding plans get all the headlines, but the real story worth telling is what engaged couples do with, for, and about each other while the plans are being made. Life is what happens when you are doing something else, they say. Engagement is what happens when everyone else is planning the wedding. Weddings are the ceremonies that launch marriages. But attention to engagements makes marriages work.

Here is a book that attends to that. It presents marriage with all its hope and promise, but also with the realistic issues that real couples face and ought to handle "now," in anticipation of marriage—not after the fact, when marriage is a given. It provides useful exercises that engage couples in mutual understanding. It faces realities of the human condition with an optimistic perspective on the sacred state of marriage. It acknowledges diversity, avoids preachiness, and provides Jewish wisdom for couples at their most opportune anticipation of happiness: engagement, betwixt and between, a creative moment to plan a brilliant future.

This is a book for such planning. I am delighted to write its introduction. I welcome its readers into the world where every wonderful thing is worth contemplating; and just maybe, all of them are possible.

Rabbi Lawrence A. Hoffman

Introduction

It is as hard for couples to come together as it was for the
Red Sea to be split.

BT *Sotah* 2a

Once you get the ring everything changes. You don't think
it is going to change, but all of a sudden your life becomes
totally different.

Rita, Paramus, New Jersey

David and Vera met during their junior year of college. As the sixth
anniversary of their first date approached, each of them was thinking
that the time to get engaged had arrived. For months, both had been
dropping hints that they were prepared to make a more serious commitment. On the night of their anniversary, Vera was trying not to think
too much about whether David was going to propose. But it was nearly
impossible. So she decided to make a list of all the reasons why she
loved him. After dinner, she gave it to him as her anniversary gift. David
gave her a gift certificate for a facial.

Despite its awkward beginning, the evening ended as they had both
hoped it would. David did manage to ask Vera to marry him that night,
and she happily accepted. They sat up all night, unable to sleep. They
kept staring at the ring, then at each other, then back at the ring.
Wordlessly, they kept asking each other: "Are we really going to do
this?" The next day, as if there had been no doubts in their minds, they
called their parents and friends with news of their engagement. After
about a week, they realized it was time to start taking care of some of

the details of the wedding: the place, the caterer, the time, the food, the rabbi, the flowers, the accommodations for out-of-town guests—the list went on and on. Somehow, though, in the rush of details, they both felt there was something missing. As David put it, "Getting engaged is sort of dangerous. You make the most important decision of your life, and then you spend all this time on details, details, details; you forget about the big picture."

The big picture is what this book is all about. This is not a guide about how to plan the details of the wedding. It is not about how to shop for the rings, how to throw the perfect wedding shower, or how to choose a florist. This book is about starting a life together, about planning for the big picture.

Engagement is a big, brand-new step. It may be exhilarating or terrifying, or even both at once. Too often, the meaning of this important time gets lost in the shuffle of the wedding plans. While the period of time prior to a wedding can be stressful, it can also be a period of real holiness.

This book is for people who wish to transform their engagement from simply a period of planning details to a meaningful passage in their lives. It is a guide for couples to embark on a journey, a journey that utilizes the wisdom and traditions of Judaism in order to strengthen their relationship and begin building their life together.

In helping you plan for the big picture, this book has three strands. One focuses on the uniqueness of becoming engaged and the various parts of your lives that are in flux. The second focuses on issues that most couples face during this time, such as dealing with money, creating intimacy, discussing spirituality, dealing with in-laws, and becoming a family. Each issue is presented through contemporary vignettes and insights from Jewish sources and is accompanied by exercises and questions for the two of you to reflect on and discuss. Exploring these issues during your period of engagement, will help to establish a framework for open and honest communication that you will carry with you into your marriage.

The third strand of the book focuses on Jewish engagement rituals. Through the ages, Jews have created a variety of rituals to mark this momentous milestone in their lives. By learning more about these rituals and their meanings, perhaps you will be inspired to find a spiritually and personally meaningful way to celebrate your own engagement.

In this book you will be introduced to examples drawn from biblical and classic rabbinic texts in order to gain insights into the nature of your relationship through a specifically Jewish frame. Traditional Jewish writings are based on stories and laws found in the Torah. In the often enigmatic and inconclusive statements in the Torah, each generation of Jews has sought teachings for their lives in countless centuries and locales. Starting with the stories of the Torah, Jews have engaged in the ongoing process of asking questions about the text, creating stories, or midrash, to fill in gaps, using the texts as a way to teach and learn about our lives as human beings and our relationship to God and the world. In addition to becoming familiar with Jewish stories and teachings, we invite you to actively participate in this uniquely Jewish process of personal meaning making, by culling the stories for their relevance for you, as individuals and as a couple.

Note

Before you begin, there are two important things you should know. First, until 1972, all rabbinic stories and generally accepted interpretations were the products of men. Second, the Bible and traditional rabbinic texts assumed that all human beings were heterosexual. Therefore, all traditional stories about meetings, courtships, and long-term committed sexual relationships were written by men and spoke about relationships between men and women. While acknowledging these realities about the inherited tradition, this book neither embraces nor reflects the same worldview or assumptions. Traditional stories will be told in their original forms but interpreted in an intentionally broad and inclusive manner—to offer insights and lessons for couples of all sexual orientations. Also, contemporary midrashim and stories will be included to highlight the ways in which the stories we tell and the insights they offer reflect the world in which we live.

PART I

Getting Started

Meeting at the Well

Birth is a beginning
And death a destination.
From childhood to maturity
And life is a journey:
Youth to age;
From innocence to awareness
And ignorance to knowing.

Alvin I. Fine, *Gates of Prayer*
(New York: CCAR Press, 1975)

Sadie arrived at Ellis Island with her dowry in hand, a few down pillows and some embroidered linen. She had sailed for days to a country she had never seen, to marry a man she had never met. Her parents had written back and forth to him in America for months. They had received lovely gifts, a photograph of their son-in-law-to-be, information about the type of job he held and his future plans. They were satisfied. From a distance, his parents seemed nice; they knew and liked his cousins, who lived in their town. They were good people. They were sure he would treat her well. Her parents assured her that people had married in this way "as far back as people can remember." As she left the processing station at Ellis Island, Sadie saw many men waiting outside. She had no idea which one was Harry, her husband-to-be. She had his picture, and he had hers. As she scanned the faces of all the men, one man with a bouquet of flowers shyly approached her and bowed. A few weeks later, they were married.

In the liturgy of a traditional *b'rit milah*, or circumcision ritual, the parents are reminded of their important parental responsibilities: "As he has entered into the Covenant of Abraham, so may he enter into the study of Torah, the blessing of marriage, and the practice of goodness." Sadie's parents, and those of her husband-to-be, were doing right by their children. They had sought an appropriate match. Like countless generations before them, these parents desired a match to someone with *yichus*, "good lineage"— often defined among Jews as a combination of wealth, learning, and health. While Sadie's marriage was arranged by her family, many marriages were arranged by a professional, recognized, paid match-maker—in Yiddish, a *shadchan*.

Whether with the aid of a *shadchan* or through personal connections, parents were responsible for finding a good *shiduch* for their children. Interestingly, the word *shiduchin* literally means "tranquility" in Aramaic. One medieval rabbi suggested that the term "tranquility" refers to the tranquility the bride found in her husband's home. Others have suggested it is the tranquility found by the parents upon arranging a successful marriage for a child.

Why wouldn't such tranquility be possible with any match? Well, a lot was at stake. And a lot of details that could be a source of struggle and conflict needed to be worked out.

A *shiduch* did not just happen. Extensive negotiations over *tachlis*, "things of substance," took place. A *shiduch* was an agreement between the parents of the couple. The parents went back and forth, articulating a wide range of issues. What assets would the bride bring to the relationship? What would the value and contents of the dowry be? What monetary obligations would the husband or his family make to the bride and to her parents, both before the marriage and after? What price would the groom pay for the bride? When would the marriage take place? What would the groom's status be at the time of the marriage: was he a student, was he new to his profession, or was he established in his profession, with a certain amount or type of assets? If the husband was a student and not yet able to support a family, who would support them? How long would the bride wait for her husband or husband-to-be to complete his studies? While he was a student (assuming he studied away from home), how frequently would they see each other? Where would they live? Who would pay for the wedding? Where would the wedding take place? And if the conditions were not met, how would the wronged family's suffering and losses be compensated? All of these were questions that needed answers.

While the couple's lives were the main focus of the discussions, they rarely participated in them. This was a matter for their parents, not them. At the end of the negotiations, a detailed document was prepared, articulating all of the agreed upon conditions, called in Hebrew, *t'nai-im*. The responsible parties (usually the father or other male relative of each member of the couple) publicly signed the *t'nai-im*. Families and friends witnessed the occasion and celebrated it.

A New World, A New Approach

Only a small percentage of the Jewish world still depends on matchmakers and arranged marriages. As arranged marriages waned, the formal documents that laid out the negotiated conditions of the wedding fell out of use as well. While a *t'nai-im* document containing preconditions for your wedding may seem antiquated, taking time during your engagement period to negotiate some of what you anticipate in your marriage can be invaluable. As rabbis, we often counsel couples who married without ever really honestly and earnestly discussing their expectations for their shared future. By using the exercises in this book, you will have an opportunity to explore and discuss these issues, so that you can deepen your relationship as you prepare for your life together.

The chapters in this book encourage you to seriously consider the conditions—*t'nai-im*—and expectations that are the basis for your contemplating marriage. They provide you with a framework for addressing the issues that many contemporary couples face, everything from whether or not you want to have children, to how you and your partner deal with anger, to whether you want to keep kosher, to what surnames you will use, to how you will express your sexual desires, to how you will handle your finances. While such issues often get pushed off center stage as weddings are planned, by addressing these issues now you can learn a great deal about yourselves and each other and get your marriage off to a good start.

Many couples find it helpful to have a rabbi or cantor facilitate these discussions. They benefit from the input and structure that a religious leader can offer. Discussing the *tachlis*, the matters of substance, of your own lives, isn't easy. But, it is essential if you are going to comfortably and happily continue to journey together. Also, by completing the sections in each chapter entitled "Conditions and Promises," you will have the ingredients for compiling a personally meaningful set of contemporary *t'nai-im* for yourselves, if this is something you would like to do.

Getting to know and understand another human being can be exciting, exhilarating, and full of surprises. To successfully embark on this journey together, you will need to develop your own meaningful modes of communication. No two people's lives are identical. We are each the product of complex biological, social, and environmental systems. Even the people with whom we feel the greatest closeness and understanding will experience and interpret moments and relationships in their lives in their own unique ways. Recognizing, understanding, and honoring similarities and differences are at the heart of all loving, enduring relationships. As you begin to look at your relationship as one that will grow and endure, learning to communicate clearly with each other is essential. Differences need not lead to irreparable divisions and breaks. Rather, they can be opportunities for each of you to grow as individuals and for you to grow as a couple.

Your Life Journeys

Each of you has been on a sacred journey since your birth. You have been students of life—learning about love, dreaming dreams, and making plans. You have experienced joy and pain, confusion and clarity, success and failure, love and hate. You have known people you trusted and people you feared. And you have learned about relationships and marriages through the examples of countless lives.

Meetings: The Well

> Three met their marriage partners at the well—Isaac, Jacob, and Moses.
>
> *Sh'mot Rabbah* 1:32

In biblical times, everyone's personal journey led to the well. At this simple gathering place, everyone in the community came to draw water for themselves, for their families, and for their flocks. During the slow process of filling their jugs, there was time to schmooze, time to socialize, to meet someone, to get to know someone, or to catch up with old friends. If you were looking for someone in particular and didn't know where to find him or her, odds were someone at the well could help you. And once having met someone at the well, it was possible to get a first impression, to decide if you wanted to get to know a person better. It is no surprise that the most common place for our biblical ancestors to meet was at the well.

For us, there is no single, central place where meetings and introductions predictably occur. And yet, people do manage to meet each other: at summer camps, at college parties, at the synagogue, at work, at the gym, or even on-line. People establish connections that lead to relationships and even lifelong commitments. Think about it. Somehow the two of you met and somehow your meeting led you to where you are today. The path from a first meeting to a commitment is rarely predictable or linear. As the following biblical and personal stories show, this is not a new phenomenon. In fact, it is as old as some of the world's earliest recorded stories.

Moses: He Didn't Really Notice Her

When Moses arrived at the well, he noticed the groups gathered there but was seemingly unaware of the individuals.

> Now the priest of Midian had seven daughters. They came to draw water, and filled the troughs to water their father's flock; but the shepherds came and drove them off. Moses rose to their defense and watered their flock.
>
> Exodus 2:16–17

His future wife was among the seven, but neither one paid particular attention to the other. They did not even ask each other's name.

Jacob: With No Expectations, Love at First Sight

Jacob met Rachel after he had been at the well for a short time. He had come looking for Rachel's father, his uncle, Laban, not for her.

[Jacob] said to them, "Do you know Laban son of Nahor?" And they said, "Yes, we do." He continued, "Is he well?" They answered, "Yes, he is; and there is his daughter Rachel, coming with the flock."

Genesis 29:5–6

While he was still speaking with them, Rachel came with her father's flock, for she was a shepherdess. And when Jacob saw Rachel, . . . Jacob went up and rolled the stone off the mouth of the well, and watered the flock of his uncle Laban. Then Jacob kissed Rachel and broke into tears.

Genesis 29:9–11

For Jacob, there was immediate recognition and attraction. It was love at first sight!

Isaac: He Knew What I Was Looking for and Made Sure We Met

Isaac was not at the well. His father's servant Eleazar was there instead, having been sent to find a wife for Isaac.

And it came to pass, . . . behold, Rebekah came out . . . and the servant ran to meet her and said, "Let me, I beg you, drink a little water from your water jar." And she said, "Drink my lord." And she hurried, and let down her water jar upon her hand, and gave him drink. And when she had finished giving him drink, she said, "I will draw water for your camels also, until they have finished drinking."

Genesis 24:15–19

Eleazar, having known Isaac for years, knew that this was the woman for him.

Ann: Who Knew I'd Meet the Love of My Life?

At age 94, Ann's memory isn't what it used to be. But when she recalls the day she met Leon, her wistful voice becomes animated, and her face brightens. "I'll never forget it! My older sister, June, had a date with a *college* man. We were all so excited for her. Well, he asked her if she had a friend who could go out with a friend of his. And she said, 'Yes.' But, it wasn't a friend at all that she was going to bring. It was me, her sister. And so, we went on this double date, back in 1926. I was nervous. Blind dates, you know. But, there was no need to be. Leon was cute and funny. And that was that. I just went on a lark. Who knew I'd meet the love of my life?"

Jamie: A Jewish Singles Event—No Way!

Jamie had argued incessantly with her mother about meeting someone. It wasn't that she wasn't interested. It was just that she didn't want her mother to be meddling in her life. She was in her twenties, living on her own and working at a job she loved. Finally, to end the conversation, she promised her mother that she would go to a Jewish singles event. She cajoled her friend Liz into dropping by with her, on the way to a movie. Jokingly, they agreed that if either of them met someone, the other should feel free to leave. Almost immediately, Jon came over to talk. When it was time to go to the movie, Jamie chose to stay, and Liz left alone. Ultimately, staying to get to know Jon was an incredibly important decision for Jamie. They eventually got married.

Julie and Nomi: We Knew It Was the Start of a Wonderful Friendship, but Who Knew That . . .

Julie and Nomi were at their mutual friend Debbie's for dinner. They'd never met before. Conversation over dinner was comfortable and free-flowing, nothing strained and nothing noteworthy. While Debbie responded to a lengthy business call, Julie and Nomi discovered that they had gone to the same summer camp and the same college and that they shared a host of interests. At the end of the evening, they both felt they had met someone they would like to get to know better. Neither was looking for a relationship. Both were happy to have found a new friend. As Nomi said, "We knew it was the start of a wonderful friendship, but who knew we would become life partners?"

Recollecting the Journey to the Well

In the Torah, when Eleazar met Rebekah at the well, he suspected that she was the woman he was intended to bring back for Isaac.

> The man, meanwhile, stood gazing at her, silently wondering whether *Adonai* had made his errand successful or not.
>
> Genesis 24:21

When Eleazar was offered lodging for the night with Rebekah's family, he unloaded his camels and sat down for a meal with his host. However, before eating, Eleazar insisted:

> "I will not eat until I have told my tale."
>
> Genesis 24:33

And so he explained how he came to the well and every detail of his interactions and conversations as well. He also offered his explanation of how he came to find the woman for whom he was looking.

Eleazar's storytelling is not unique. In fact, it highlights the fact that telling the stories of our first encounters has been going on since time immemorial. Somehow, when we announce that we have met a new person or when we share that we are engaged, the first questions our friends, acquaintances, and families ask is "So, how did you meet?" Take a moment to think back to your well, the place where you met.

Your Journeys to and beyond the Well

Now that you have recalled the circumstances of your meeting, consider the history of your relationship as a couple. Whether you have been together months or years, your relationship has its own history. How you first met, your first holiday together, your first kiss, these are all parts of your history. One of the ways you can learn a great deal about yourselves and your relationship is through mapping your history. This involves taking time to review your relationship history and trying to map it graphically. Besides giving you what might be an interesting visual perspective, this activity can facilitate a helpful conversation about the past. By exploring your shared past, you can gain clarity and greater understanding about yourselves and your relationship. Couples who have taken the time to map their relationship have inevitably felt rewarded by the experience of reviewing their relationship and highlighting certain moments as milestones on their map. An essential part of this process is becoming aware of the differences in the ways each of you describes both the moments you include and your experiences of them. Challenge yourselves to acknowledge, accept, and validate those differences.

You may find that you are more comfortable engaging in this exercise with a rabbi or therapist guiding you through it and any subsequent discussions engendered by it.

We would suggest one way of mapping out your relationship is by graphing the high and low points. Put time on one axis, and on the other axis put the quality of the experience.

Exercise 1. Mapping Your Relationship

PART I

Separately, map or graph out your experiences.
 Consider placing the following relationship milestones on your map as well as any others you deem important:

Your first meeting
The decision to see each other exclusively
Vacationing together
Meeting each other's friends
Meeting each other's colleagues
Meeting each other's families
Celebrating a holiday together
Making financial decisions together
Any breakups and subsequent reunions (many couples have at least
  one such occurrence)

Talking about a long-term future (think of specific examples)
Moving in together

PART II

Share your map with your partner. Describe why you chose each moment.
Pay attention to different choices you made and why you made those
choices.

PART III

Give each other time to comment and respond.

Remember: You have lived through the same moments and
events, but each of you has perceived them and experienced them
differently. Becoming aware of and sensitized to your differences is
an essential part of deepening and expanding your relationship.

PART IV

Together, find a way to create a single map that accurately includes all of
the points of your relationship history, somehow indicating the importance
the various steps and stages have had for each of you.

An Engagement Ritual: The Blessings of the Well

Some people liken the decision to make a long-term commitment to
another person as reaching a mountaintop, while others simply wake up
one morning and realize that it is the natural next step. Some couples
surprise each other with gifts to mark the occasion. Some couples
decide together that they will have an engagement period in which to
work out the details of how they will tell people and when they will officially become engaged. Others make elaborate plans for a formal
announcement and exchange of rings or other tokens.

Most engagement parties do not offer a spiritual way of marking this
important transition. The following ritual can provide an opportunity,

for you and for others, to evoke blessings for this new stage of your relationship.

For the ritual, you will need a table, three cups, some water, and two chairs placed on opposite sides of the table, facing each other. You will sit in these chairs during the ritual. You can do this ritual alone or in the company of friends or family. If you choose to do it with others, invite them to sit in a circle around the two of you. If you are alone, one of you will read the following. If friends or relatives are present, ask one of them to read the following:

When Jacob met Rachel at the well, the midrash says that the water of the well miraculously surged up to meet Jacob and flooded out over the top of the well and over the entire town as a blessing of water for the entire community.

Each of you take a moment to share how your life has been overflowing with blessings since you met.

If friends are present, ask them to share how they feel their lives and the lives of their communities have been blessed since you became a couple.

Each of you, in turn, takes some water from the cup in front of you and puts it in the empty middle cup, until it overflows.

Continue with the following (if you are alone, you can say it yourselves; if you are with friends, a friend can ask the questions):

The question asked of Rebekah by her brother and father
(in Genesis 24:58)

As you (we) set out on the next stage of your (our) journey,

[For a man to a woman:]

Hateilchi im ha-ish hazeh?

הֲתֵלְכִי עִם־הָאִישׁ הַזֶּה?

Will you go with this man?

[For a man to a man:]

Hateileich im ha-ish hazeh?

הֲתֵלֵךְ עִם־הָאִישׁ הַזֶּה?

Will you go with this man?

[For a woman to a man:]

Hateileich im ha-ishah hazot?

הֲתֵלֵךְ עִם־הָאִשָּׁה הַזֹּאת?

Will you go with this woman?

[For a woman to a woman:]

Hateilchi im ha-ishah hazot?

הֲתֵלְכִי עִם־הָאִשָּׁה הַזֹּאת?

Will you go with this woman?

In response to the question, you each respond:

Eileich!

אֵלֵךְ!

I will go!

After each of you responds, each of you, in turn, drinks half the contents of the middle cup.

Then, say together:

May our relationship be a constant well reviving our spirits, overflowing with blessing.

2

Make Me a Perfect Match:
Expectations and Fears

> Matchmaker, matchmaker make me a match, find me a find,
> catch me a catch. Matchmaker, matchmaker look through
> your book, and make me a perfect match.
>
> *Fiddler on the Roof*

As you begin to explore your relationship, consider what expectations of a marriage partner you had previously—what type of person he/she would be, what he/she would do for a living, what kind of friends he/she would have. The expectations each of you had of whom your life partner was going to be have a tremendous impact on your relationship. During one premarital counseling session, David put the issue this way:

> It's when we're late getting somewhere that we run into problems. I'll be relaxed and say things like, "It's okay, we're on Jewish time," or "It's just not a big deal if we're late to the doctor/movie/haircutter/ name your appointment." She'll get tense, nervous, and irritable. When I used to think about getting married, I used to think about marrying this sweet person who saw the world exactly as I did, who liked Van Morrison and Woody Allen. Who was quiet like I am, and laid back like I am. Who when we were late would say things like, "It's no big deal." Well, now I'm marrying Kara, who does not listen to Van Morrison, thinks most of Woody Allen is narcisstic, and who gets worried and neurotic when we're late or things aren't going as planned.

Kara and David were together for five years before they got engaged. It had been a long courtship precisely because of their differences and their efforts to try to navigate them. David said that one of the most important things for him to keep in mind was that it was precisely his own expectations of who he was going to marry that sometimes tripped him up in dealing with the actual person, Kara. David said:

> Sometimes I won't accept how Kara is acting, because I'll think about how I'd like her to act. And I can tell her that. But at some point I have to recognize that she's not going to be who I want her to be all the time, and it's probably good for me that she's not. Sometimes I probably need someone to tell me it's not okay to be late to everything.

Many people find that the person they end up with is not the type of person they had always presumed they would be with. Now that you are on the threshold of marriage, you probably recognize how your partner compares to your earlier expectations. You always thought you would end up with someone fiery and passionate, but you ended up with someone more passive and even-keeled; you imagined that you would marry a bohemian artist, and you are with a corporate lawyer, or vice versa.

The following passage is a suggestion from the Talmud on the characteristics one should look for in a partner.

> Our masters taught: Let a man always sell all he has in order to marry the daughter of a disciple of the wise. If he does not find the daughter of a disciple of the wise, let him marry the daughter of one of the notables of the generation. If he does not find the daughter of one of the notables of the generation, let him marry the daughter of the head of a synagogue. If he does not find the daughter of the head of a synagogue, let him marry the daughter of the collector of funds for charity. If he does not find the daughter of a collector of funds for charity, let him marry the daughter of a teacher of young children.
>
> BT *P'sachim* 49a–b

The Rabbis of the Talmud had clear ideas of the ideal marriage hierarchy. They had definable categories of the families that produced the most and the least desirable spouses. While their criteria are perhaps not yours, you have probably had a sense, articulated or not, of some of the characteristics that you expected your spouse to have.

The following exercise asks you to look back at the expectations for a future partner you held prior to this relationship. It also asks you to think about where these expectations came from. For most people, their parents' relationship remains an indelible model, for better or for worse, of what a marital relationship looks like. By gaining an understanding of the origins of your ideals and images of marriage, we hope you will be able to better understand aspects of yourself and of your own relationship with your partner.

Exercise 2. Expectations

PART I

Separately, answer the following questions:

1. At what stage of your life did you think you were going to get married?
2. Why would you get married?
3. Would it be someone Jewish?
4. Would it be someone your family knew?
5. Would it be someone who would get along with your siblings? With your friends?
6. What characteristics did you think your partner would have?
7. What new roads would open? Which old roads would come to an end?

Now share these earlier expectations with each other. Note and discuss similarities and differences.

PART II

Separately, answer the following questions:

1. What was your parents' marriage(s) like? What do you see as its strengths and weaknesses?
2. What was your position in the family? How were the roles and expectations for you similar or different from those of your siblings? Why?

3. How do you view your relationship? How is it similar or different from your parents'?
4. What factors are you aware of that have shaped your hopes and expectations for marriage?

PART III

Separately, answer the following questions:

1. How did your first impressions of each other differ from the way that your families of origin perceive you?
2. How have you gotten to know and understand yourself better through this relationship?
3. Do you expect changes or transformations to accompany your engagement? Your marriage? If so, what?

Share your responses with each other. Note the similarities and differences. Remember, no two people are alike. Relationships depend on individuals' accepting and respecting the similarities and differences they have with others.

PART IV

Share your thoughts regarding each other's responses.

1. What surprised you?
2. What touched you?
3. What annoyed you?

At the Crossroads: Fears and Doubts— "Life is Not a Stupid Bridal Magazine!"

Love alone dominates fear.

Zohar, Exodus, 2:216a

Being engaged is an incredibly scary time, because you are just totally fearful of having made the wrong decision; and, it's the whole life thing, forever, that's it, no going back.

Jacob, 35, New York City

Jane remembers that she was not exactly the blissful bride, "I had anxiety about our engagement and our relationship, and I had anxiety about our actual wedding day. Unfortunately, I felt like I did not want to share my doubts, even with my close friends. People would think badly of me and of my relationship. I did not want people to think that I did not really love my fiancé, and I also worried that if I talked about my fears out loud, that it would magnify them." Jane couldn't understand why she didn't feel joyful as her wedding approached. Jane had been picturing her wedding day since she was young. She had always imagined a perfect day with a purely joyous engagement leading up to it. And all those bridal magazines she read reinforced this idea. "I got all those magazines that brides get. And there were all of these beautiful pictures of people with beautiful smiles, looking beautifully serene. But, sometimes life is not a stupid bridal magazine!"

In truth, real life is never a bridal magazine. It has highs and lows. It has its moments of certainty as well as moments of anxiety and confusion. Not every moment of engagement is easy or necessarily happy. In fact, because it is a major transitional time for you, your relationship with each other and your relationships with family and friends are all in flux. This reality can cause some people to feel anxious and others to become very fearful. For some, the concerns that come to the fore never shake their firm sense that they have found the person with whom they wish to make a life. For others, the question "Do I really want to marry *this* person?" looms large.

Ideally, serious questions about the viability of your match should precede your discussions about marriage. Making an enduring commitment to another human being is a life-altering act. Deciding to make such a commitment signifies that you have come to realize that though your partner cannot satisfy all of your needs, nor all of your desires, that, indeed, she or he gives you *enough* peace, satisfies *enough* of your desires and needs, to be a real partner for you.

As you read and work your way through this book, reflect on the teachings. Take time to answer the questions and do the exercises. Plan for the rituals. They will provide you with an opportunity to discuss your hopes and expectations, and confront and work through some of your concerns, so that you can make a long-term commitment to each other, with your eyes open and with as few secrets or surprises as possible.

If you find that yours are not just anxieties, but real fears and dread, put this book aside for a while; decide if you should be talking about a shared future at all. If you are questioning the wisdom of your decision, for your own sake and the sake of your partner, do not ignore it. Fear can be an important warning sign that you are not emotionally prepared to move forward as planned. In the long run, postponing a wedding and/or seeking professional counsel can save you and many other people from experiencing hurt and confusion. Rabbis, couples and family therapists, and many other professionals are ready and able to work with engaged couples. Seeking help and guidance has helped many couples discern the viability of their relationship and their readiness to make a commitment. Sometimes just talking to a third party can help you gain clarity. Many couples find that their relationships and commitments are stronger as a result. Others find that there is good reason to be fearful and have the support to take the time they need to address their fears. Do what you can so that your fears today do not lead to anger, frustration, pain, and disappointment in the future.

PART II

Issues

3

Intimacy

Sh'lom Bayit: Peace in the Home

Rabban Shimon ben Gamliel said: Those who cause peace to reign
in their house are regarded as though they have caused peace
between every individual in Israel, and those who cause jealousy
and contention to reign in their house are regarded as though they
have caused jealousy and contention to reign in all of Israel.

Avot D' Rabbi Natan 28:3

The rabbis of every generation have understood how hard it is for
human beings to develop and maintain intimacy, even with those they
love and those to whom they feel a bond and commitment. There is so
much to negotiate. Time commitments, career goals, not to mention
sharing space, friends, and family with another human being who
thinks differently, feels differently, acts differently, and reacts differently, are constant challenges for contemporary couples. Fortunately,
despite such challenges, relationships can grow and flourish through
sharing, trusting, and understanding. Intimacy grows and deepens as
two lives become intertwined.

Generations of rabbis and Jews have believed that true intimacy is
linked to a home where there is *sh'lom bayit,* "peace in the home."
Sh'lom bayit does not mean that things will always be peaceful. Rather,
it means finding ways to communicate with each other that are clear
and honest, that are ever conscious of and concerned with protecting
each other, with not harming each other through words or actions. As
long as you are together, you will be engaged in a process of trying to
understand each other's needs and modes of expression, of negotiating

ways to honor and respect each other's differences. These will be fundamental to your finding a sense of peace in your relationship, so that that peace can pervade your home.

Emotional Intimacy

When Linda was playing the piano, she completely lost track of time. She would get lost in the music, unaware of the world around her. Jeff enjoyed the music but always reminded her, in advance, of the things they planned or needed to do, hoping that she would just play a single song or not sit down at the piano at all. He always felt guilty interrupting her, so she never knew how frustrated he became when she would play right through a TV show they had said they would watch together or the hour to get to the early showing of a movie. He knew Linda didn't mean to miss other things; she just got totally absorbed in her music.

Hank was single-minded about getting his business off the ground. Margie had admired his perseverance as he struggled to put himself through business school. She had even encouraged him to dream about the type of career he would love to pursue. Never did she imagine that his dream would lead him to start his own business from scratch. Instead of getting out of debt when he finished school, they went further into debt. While he was in business school, she felt she never got to see him. Now, she dreamed about those days. Compared to the present, they saw each other all of the time then. The business demanded all of his time and energy. He promised that it would change as soon as the business took off. And she truly wished for the best. But, much of the time she was lonely and frustrated by the life they were living. Imagining their future, she didn't feel as hopeful as Hank.

During her residency, Emily had worked crazy hours. That didn't bother Alan. He knew it was for a limited period of time. They spoke often about the type of schedule Emily would keep once she was settled into emergency medicine. She'd work in an ER four days a week, leaving time to be a mom who could go to soccer games and be present in her family's life. However, during their engagement, Emily was at work constantly; they jokingly referred to the hospital as her home, and their home as her guesthouse. It was frustrating for both of them to be apart so much.

Marion was devastated by the news that her mother had cancer. When she told Jeff, he took her in his arms and held her. She prattled on about the options that were available to her mother. Jeff listened for a while and then interrupted her. He looked her in the eye and said, "Shsh. I've never felt your body so tense before. Let yourself cry. Maybe it will help." No one had ever made such an offer to her. She was always the strong one. She was always there for other people. She wanted desperately to cry. But, she'd never before let herself cry in front of anybody else. She'd never cried before in someone else's arms. Marion took a deep breath, hoping to hold back the tears. Instead, they started to flow. Jeff didn't pull back. He didn't tell her to be strong. He just held her tightly as she cried.

Aaron spent his professional life mediating disputes. He was constantly exposed to the verbal abuse and outrageous hyperbole of people who were trying to prove each other wrong. In his personal life, he was always careful about what he said. He knew that his opinions of the people with whom he worked were negative. He feared that if he shared his real, negative feelings with anyone, their opinion of him would plummet. He came home one night and couldn't contain his distress. Marla asked him what was wrong. He hesitated. Marla loved him. What did that mean? Could he trust her with what he saw as his darker side? Would she still love him if he told her what he was thinking and feeling? He couldn't be sure. He'd never had success before. But something inside pushed him to talk openly with Marla. Rather than running away or telling him he was a horrible person, she was attentive and supportive, even surprised that he had been so uncertain about her response.

Letting the person you love know how you feel, while being cognizant of yours and your partner's feelings, is no easy feat. Learning how to be honest and caring, critical and loving, and open to loving criticism are all signs of trusting yourself with your partner and trusting your partner with you. Committing yourselves to establishing this kind of intimacy can be hard. But failing to do so can have devastating effects on your relationship. As the Talmud says,

> When our love was strong, we could have made our bed on a sword's blade; now when it has become weak, a bed of sixty cubits is not large enough for us.
>
> BT *Sanhedrin* 7a

Ideally, as your lives become more intertwined, your desire to communicate and share can grow.

> A midrash asks, why does the biblical verse "Adam knew his wife yet more" [Genesis 4:25] say 'yet more'? It offers the answer, Adam's desire for his wife was increased by much more desire than before; formerly he had felt no desire to be with her when he did not see his wife; but now he felt desire to be with her whether he saw her or not.
>
> *B'reishit Rabbah* 23:5

As your love and relationship grow, as your sense of intimacy deepens, your desire to be with each other so that you can share with each other can deepen as well.

Anger

Negotiating and meshing different ways of expressing, responding to, and interpreting anger are a frequent challenge for couples. However, though it can be scary, learning to express a wide range of emotions, including anger, is necessary for the two of you to share true emotional intimacy.

Neil's parents rarely fought, at least not publicly. Instead, they would actively ignore each other and silently seethe. No one ever raised a voice in anger while he was growing up. Rather, hushed tones and silence signaled danger and transgression. Members of Joan's family, on the other hand, would scream and yell whenever they were angry, hurt, or confused. The first few times Neil visited Joan's parents' home, he left visibly shaken, convinced that he never wanted to return. He shared with Joan his sense that each time he left, he felt like he was emerging from World War III . . . almost. Almost, because even though bombs went off sporadically, there would be calm and even joking in their aftermath. When Neil and Joan were angry with each other, their different family patterns became evident. Neil got exceedingly quiet and sulked when he was angry, while Joan screamed. Neil's sulking unnerved Joan, while Joan's yelling unnerved Neil. They each thought the other had a problem expressing anger. In truth they both had a problem; neither had ever told the other how their partner's way of expressing anger made them feel.

The first time Jon and Barbara got into a big fight, Barbara cried and shook, while Jon raised his voice and screamed. Barbara's tears angered Jon. "If we're going to fight," he said, "then we both should use words." Barbara was so overwhelmed with fear and rage that no words would come. She'd never had someone she loved scream at her with such intensity. Jon, frustrated, said that he was going to go for a walk to cool off. He hoped that when he got back, Barbara would be ready to talk. As the door shut, Barbara couldn't control her sobs. Jon had just walked out on her. How were they ever going to work this out? When Jon came back an hour later, he was calm, clearheaded, and ready to talk. Barbara was stunned by the change that he'd undergone and had no idea of how to deal with it. Gingerly, she began to discuss with Jon what had transpired.

Every human being occasionally feels anger and develops a way to express it. The same can be said for every couple. As you learn to live with each other, as you look to share a future together, it is important for you to appreciate and understand the distinct ways that each of you expresses anger and the ways in which you as a couple handle annoying and frustrating situations and people. There is a rabbinic expression that the wise man's wisdom deserts him when he is angry. Care must be taken to express anger in such a way that you will not be destroying *sh'lom bayit* in the process.

Exercise 3. Exploring Anger

Discuss each of the following questions with your partner:

1. How do you deal with anger?
2. How comfortable are you with the ways you deal with anger?
3. Is your manner similar to that of other members of your family of origin?
4. How did you feel as a child when your parents expressed anger toward you?
5. Are you aware of responding differently to specific expressions of anger?

6. How is your way of dealing with anger similar to and/or different from your partner's?
7. How have you negotiated your differences?

L'shon Hatov *and* L'shon Hara

Jewish tradition has always been sensitive to the impact of how we speak to or about another person. It teaches that the timing and tone of one's communication can either maintain or disrupt *sh'lom bayit* and emotional intimacy. It divides speaking into two main categories: *l'shon hara*, "bad speech," and *l'shon hatov*, "good speech." The Rabbis define *l'shon hara* as gossiping or speaking poorly about someone, and *l'shon hatov* as speaking well of someone. Throughout much of recorded history, Jews lived in small, sometimes enclosed and isolated communities. Under these circumstances, it is no surprise that the rabbis frequently cautioned against gossip and idle chatter. They understood that a few negative words about someone's character did irreparable damage and a few negative words about someone's business endangered a person's livelihood.

Even smaller than the communities of our ancestors is your home. Peace was maintained in our ancestors' communities when people learned to use their power of speech cautiously and wisely. This same wisdom applies to you in your home. As our tradition teaches, words can be dangerous weapons.

> Two rabbis were arguing about which weapon most resembled words. The first rabbi asked, "Why not . . . a sword for example?" "Because," answered the second, "if a man unsheathes his sword to kill his friend, and the friend begs for mercy, the man may be mollified and return his sword to its scabbard. But an arrow, once it is shot, can never be returned, no matter how much one wants to."
>
> *Midrash Sachar Tov* 120

In some ways relationships constantly test our ability to use words wisely. Not everything on the tip of a tongue must be said. Harsh remarks and words of criticism can often remain unuttered. Learning when to intervene and share words of criticism or concern with your mate is important if you are to establish and maintain *sh'lom bayit*.

Mindy could see how uncomfortable Ben was when Jay asked about the brace on his knee. His face had scrunched up. He fumbled for words. Jay shifted from one foot to another. Finally, Ben said something, and the conversation moved on. Mindy knew that Ben would feel even more uncomfortable if she brought up the subject while they were out with friends. But she also knew that Ben expected and wanted her to be honest about how she perceived him, about how he presented himself to others. So as they drove home, she asked Ben if he knew why he had been so uncomfortable, if he had been aware of the facial expressions he had made and the way in which he had made a simple, potentially brief exchange longer and more uncomfortable than it needed to be.

Bob had been telling Marcy for weeks that he found the way that she twirled her hair while she was thinking absolutely annoying. She had been trying hard to become more aware of the times that she did it and to stop herself. While they were out to dinner with friends, Rich asked her a question. She paused and began to twirl her hair. Bob tilted his head, trying to catch her eye to signal her to stop. Marcy missed it entirely. Bob then reached across the table, grabbed her hand, and said, "I told you how annoying I find that!" The conversation immediately came to a halt. Marcy was embarrassed and humiliated. Bob picked up the conversation, as if nothing had happened. When they finally got home, Marcy told Bob that she had wanted to leave the restaurant and him at that moment. But she didn't want to embarrass him the way he had embarrassed her.

What to say, how to say it, and when to say it are certainly not new concerns. They are as old as the Bible itself. Rabbi Telushkin teaches, in *Words That Hurt, Words That Heal*, that even King David and his wife Michal had to learn about communicating with each other. David and Michal's father had been enemies for a long time. In fact, he and Michal could only marry once Michal helped David escape from her father, who had threatened to kill him. Their love, however, could not endure Michal's criticism of David. On the momentous day when David returned the Holy Ark, the most sacred object in ancient Israelite life, to Jerusalem, he was overcome with joy and danced wildly. Michal, watching from a window, was disgusted. When David came inside she said, "Didn't the king of Israel do himself honor today—exposing himself . . . as one of the riffraff might expose himself?" (II Samuel 6:20). David responded by saying, "It was before *Adonai*, who chose me instead of your father and all his family [that I danced]."

Michal had concerns about the propriety of David's dancing. Likening him to riffraff made it impossible for him to hear her real concerns for him and his station. Rather than remaining silent or responding to her concerns directly, David struck out in anger, attacking her father and her family. So devastating was this exchange for their relationship, that the Rabbis understood Michal's inability to later have children as a result of their never having been intimate again.

There will be times when you are tired or in a bad mood and just being available to your partner, never mind responding positively, will be a serious challenge. Finding ways to communicate with your partner about the things or people affecting your mood can prevent your partner from taking your inaccessibility personally.

Just as negative words can be terribly disruptive to *sh'lom bayit*, so can it be strengthened by positive words. Day to day, we often forget the positive power of our words. We neglect to share verbally our sense of gratitude for our partner, our sense of love and connection, our sense of pride, or our feelings of encouragement. Somehow, we assume that our partner knows what we feel and think and that words are thus unnecessary.

> One day, Rabbi Jack Riemer conducted a funeral at a cemetery. After the service everyone left except the Rabbi and the mourning husband. After some time Rabbi Riemer approached the husband and encouraged him to go home.
>
> The man waved him away. "You don't understand, I loved my wife." "I am sure you did," the Rabbi responded, "but you have been here a long time and you should go now."
>
> "You don't understand, I loved my wife," the man repeated. Once more the Rabbi urged him to go.
>
> "But you don't understand," the man told the Rabbi. "I loved my wife and—and once, I almost told her."
>
> Joseph Telushkin, *Words That Hurt, Words That Heal*
> (New York: William Morrow and Company, 1996)

Exercise 4. Time and Tone

Separately, write down your answers to the following questions. Then share your answers with each other.

1. Generally, do you feel your partner lets you know what she/he is thinking or feeling?
2. Generally, do you feel your partner chooses appropriate times to express concerns and criticisms to you?
3. Can you think of a time when you felt your partner shared concerns or criticisms at an inappropriate time?
   a) How did you feel?
   b) How did you respond?
   c) How did you address it as a couple?
   d) Were you satisfied with the outcome?
4. Are you sometimes surprised or made uncomfortable by your partner's tone of voice? Give an example. Be detailed about the situation, the way you heard the tone, and your assumption about its meaning.
5. Have you found a way to let your partner know how you respond to different tones of voice?
6. Have you found a way to address issues that arise regarding tones of voice and other aspects of verbal expression?

Exercise 5. The Things You Would Like to Hear and the Things You Wanted to Say

Part I

Separately, prepare two lists of the following. Then share their contents with your partner.

1. Things you would like your partner to take the time to say or comment about.
2. Things you believe your partner would like you to take the time to say or comment about.

Part II

Separately, respond to these considerations. Do not share your answers. Keep the sheet as a reminder for yourself.

1. Think back to a moment when you had wanted to say something positive to your partner, but for some reason you didn't. Write about the incident and reflect on why you did not.
2. Think of positive and loving things that you do not normally say, but that you feel and would like to say.
3. Challenge yourself to find times to share these feelings and thoughts with your partner.

Sexual Intimacy

You might be surprised to learn that the rabbis of every generation have openly and explicitly discussed sex. The rabbis understood that sex is an essential part of being human, and they had much to teach regarding appropriate sexual behavior. The following story from the Talmud illuminates this point. In this story, a disciple hides under his teacher's bed to learn the appropriate ways of having sex. When caught, he claims that learning about sex is part of learning Torah:

> Rav Kahana once went in and hid under Rav's bed. He heard him chatting [with his wife] and joking and doing what he required [having intercourse] . . . [Rav] said to him: Kahana, are you here? Go out, because it is rude. He replied: It is a matter of Torah, and I need to learn.
>
> BT *B'rachot* 62a

Generally, the rabbis taught that sex between two appropriate partners is a mitzvah—a sacred commandment. Our notions of appropriate sexual partners have changed—we no longer prohibit a marriage between people who had once divorced each other, and we no longer accept heterosexuality as the only "norm" for humans—but we still retain the belief that sexual intimacy can be holy. As an anonymous medieval Jewish philosopher wrote:

The act of sexual union is holy and pure. Adonai created all things in accordance with God's wisdom, and whatever God created cannot possibly be shameful or angry. When a man unites with a woman [read: when appropriate spouses unite] in a spirit of holiness and purity, the Divine Presence is with them.

Iggeret HaKodesh,
(*The Holy Letter*, trans. Seymour Cohen
[Northvale, N. J.: Jason Aronson, 1976])

Sexual Communication

Tom was intrigued but uncertain about how to respond to Hannah's suggestion that they set an alarm for two hours earlier than usual so that they could make love as the sun rose. She was excited by the prospect. It would be something novel and romantic. But Tom felt sleep deprived enough as it was. Their lovemaking was good; why bother creating a new scenario? Hannah was shocked by his reaction. Here she was considering something new, and he was finding problems with it. She wanted to know why he was hesitating. And Tom was unable to find words to explain his reaction.

Lou hadn't realized that he and Tracy had gotten into a routine. They'd go out every Thursday night for a nice dinner, a time they had set aside as just theirs. After a good meal, some wine, and time away from everything, they would go home and Tracy would expect Lou to initiate some sort of sexual play. And then, most Sunday mornings, before going to brunch with friends, they would read the paper for a while and then find themselves in each other's arms. It had all become predictable, expected. The sex was good, passionate, and satisfying. But their spontaneity seemed to have been replaced by expectations. Tracy always seemed aroused and interested, but for once Lou wanted her to make a move, for *her* to choose a different time, to let him know that he was wanted and desired.

Mike loved it when Chuck wore a certain cologne. There was something about it that was a turn-on. He couldn't explain it. When he first told Chuck about it, Chuck just laughed. But, in time, Chuck came to appreciate the small and large ways that he could make sex more pleasurable for Mike. If splashing on a little cologne would help arouse Mike, then so be it.

Before you marry, you have an opportunity to communicate with one another about your sexual relationship. You can learn to openly share your desires, your hopes, your fantasies, and your expectations. Bear in mind that shifting circumstances and demands have an influence on all aspects of your life and your relationship, including your sex life. Being a good lover is far more than having good technique. It is fundamentally about communication, about being a good communicator. Sexual dialogue is not simply about what "turns us on"; it is also about fantasies, temptation, and the place of sex in an intimate relationship.

Exercise 6. Communication

Share the following with your partner:

1. One aspect of your sex life that you particularly enjoy.
2. Something that surprised you about his/her sexual habits or appetites.
3. Something that you are pleased to have learned about your own sexual habits or appetitites.

Pleasure

In *Iggeret HaKodesh*, a medieval Jewish text, we are told:

> Engage in conversation that puts her heart and mind at ease and gladdens her. Speak words which arouse her to passion, union, love, desire and eros. Speak with her words, some of love, some of erotic passion. Hurry not to arouse passion until her mood is ready; begin in love; let her [orgasm] take place first.
>
> *Iggeret HaKodesh*,
> (*The Holy Letter*, trans. Seymour Cohen
> [Northvale, N. J.: Jason Aronson, 1976])

Even in the middle ages, Jewish teachers understood that couples must work at lovemaking. They recognized that couples needed to

Fantasies

The Rabbis taught:

> There have been four women of surpassing beauty in the world—
> Sarah, Rahab, Abigail, and Esther. Our Rabbis taught: Rahab
> inspired lust by her name. Whoever says, "Rahab, Rahab," at once
> has an ejaculation. Said Rav Nachman to him: I say "Rahab,
> Rahab," and nothing happens to me! He replied: I was speaking
> of one who knows her and is intimate with her.
>
> BT *M'gillah* 15a

Rahab, a prostitute, offered safety to two of Israel's scouts before
they conquered the city of Jericho (Joshua 2). She and her presumed
beauty became fodder for generations of rabbis as they tackled questions related to lust, longing, and fantasy. They recognized that fantasy
plays a part in our sexual lives. Over your lifetimes, each of you has
gathered or generated a set of sexual fantasies and images. Figuring out
which parts of your fantasy life to share with your partner can be challenging. This is delicate territory. You want to shed light for your partner on what you experience when you are together; but you do not want
to leave your partner feeling inadequate.

The Rabbis do caution against fantasizing in inappropriate ways:

> If a woman is having intercourse with her husband while her
> thought is with another man whom she met on the road, there is
> no greater act of adultery than this.
>
> *B'midbar Rabbah* 9:34

Judaism is very aware that many people are naturally moved to sexual fantasies. However, it is quite a leap from fantasy to adultery. The
comparison above highlights one of the rabbis' primary concerns. They
feared anything that might lead to distance or distrust between two
people in a committed relationship. They recognized that it is not
always easy to avoid thinking about others, and they found merit in the
person who is able to force himself to focus solely on his partner during intercourse:

> Ima Shalom was asked: Why are your children so handsome? She
> replied: Because my husband does not cohabit with me at the
> beginning of the night or at the end of the night, but only at mid-

night. And when he cohabits with me, he uncovers a handbreadth of my body even as he covers another handbreadth, and he acts as though a demon is driving him. When I ask him, "Why at midnight?" he replies, "So that I give no thought to another woman."

BT *N'darim* 20a–b

Exercise 8. Fantasies

Part I

Reflect on the following questions privately:

1. Do you share your sexual fantasies with each other?
2. How comfortable are you sharing your sexual fantasies?
   a) What do you fear when you share or hear a sexual fantasy?
   b) What motivates you to share a sexual fantasy?
3. Do you find fantasies threatening?

Part II

If you feel comfortable doing so, share some of your fantasies with your partner.

Fidelity and Jealousy

Rabbi Yochanan said: A bachelor who lives in a large city and does not sin—the Holy One daily proclaims his virtue. Now, Rabbi Safra was just such a bachelor living in a large city. When a *Tanna* repeated Rabbi Yochanan's dictum before Rava and Rabbi Safra, Rabbi Safra's face lit up. But Rava said to him: The dictum does not apply to such as you, sir, but such as Rabbi Chanina and Rabbi Oshaya, who were cobblers in the Land of Israel and lived in the street of harlots. They made shoes for the harlots, which they would deliver to the brothel. The harlots would gaze [provocatively] at the two Sages, but the Sages would not so much as lift their eyes to look at them. Henceforth, the oath of those harlots came to be "By the life of the holy Sages of the Land of Israel."

BT *P'sachim* 113a

While Judaism demands complete fidelity in a committed relationship, (see the Ten Commandments for proof), the issue of jealousy can be much subtler yet just as threatening to a relationship.

When Don and Linda were first dating, Don loved it when Linda would wear something sexy. He got a kick out of the attention that Linda drew from other men and the clear attraction other people felt for her. Linda would flirt back a bit, but it was all part of the game. She was clearly focused on him and their relationship. Now that Don and Linda were talking about establishing a home together and planning for a lifetime, Don found he felt less and less comfortable with some of Linda's attire and her casual flirting. He wanted the internal changes in their relationship to be reflected externally as well.

Rick came into the apartment chatting about a new person at the office. He went on and on about his looks, his sense of humor, how creatively he had attacked a problem that arose in the middle of the day. Rob listened closely and responded enthusiastically . . . at first. But as Rick waxed poetic, he got scared. When Rick commented on how nice his coworker looked, Rob couldn't control himself. He interrupted Rick and told him he had heard enough. Rick always came home talking about work and truly did not understand why Rob was so upset. When he realized that Rob was jealous and afraid about his interest in this new person, Rick assured him that talk was one thing but action another. He would never be tempted by someone else!

Exercise 9. Fidelity and Jealousy

Part I. Definitions, Responses, Expectations

Separately, answer the following questions. Then share your answers with your partner.

1. How do you define infidelity?
2. What would lead you to suspect infidelity?
3. What action do you think you would take if you suspected infidelity?
4. In theory, do you think there are means for you to accept infidelity and move ahead with your relationship?

Part II. Temptation

Separately, answer the following questions. Then share your answers with your partner.

1. How do you deal with temptations that present themselves?
2. Does your partner know what things or types of people tempt you?
3. Does your partner know how you deal with temptations?
4. If your partner felt attracted to someone, would you want to know? Under what circumstances?

Public and Private

And Balaam lifted up his eyes, and he saw Israel dwelling tribe by tribe [in such a way that] he was impelled to exclaim, "The spirit of God should rest upon Israel" [Numbers 24:2]. What did he see? He saw that the entrances to Israel's tents did not face one another [thus ensuring privacy]. So he exclaimed, "These people deserve to have the Presence rest on them"

BT *Bava Batra* 60a

Jewish texts, from the Bible to the present, have dealt with issues related to public and private behaviors. While mores and expectations change, each of us defines for ourselves what feels right and acceptable. Therefore, delving into your own behavior patterns and exploring how compatible they are with your mate's are important for your ongoing sense of comfort with each other.

When Barry and Carol were out with friends, Barry would spontaneously lean over and kiss Carol. His hand would stroke her legs or run up and down her back. Carol understood these as genuine expressions of his affection for her, but they made her uncomfortable nonetheless. Rather than make her feel good, they made her feel conspicuous and uneasy. When she mentioned this to Barry, he was hurt. Carol had told him, on numerous occasions, how much she enjoyed his romantic side. Barry was confused. Why couldn't Carol simply understand and accept his loving gestures?

When Mark and Greg were with friends, they would touch each other's hand or shoulder as they spoke. They would catch each other's eyes and smile or share a wordless thought. The intimacy of their relationship lent an ease and flow to their interactions with each other and with their friends. Mark was forever stunned and drawn up short to find that a wall went up between him and Greg whenever they were with Greg's family. Greg would position himself at a physical distance that would make a simple, unpremeditated touch impossible. He would avert his eyes from Mark, making their nonverbal communication nearly impossible. Mark always felt a bit awkward with Greg's parents; Greg's distance only added to his discomfort and sense of being in an unfamiliar and inhospitable environment.

Exercise 10. Public and Private Boundaries

Separately, answer the following questions. Then share your answers with your partner.

1. How do you share intimacies in public?
2. How does your partner express intimacy and closeness in public?
3. Have your partner's public displays of affection ever crossed a boundary for you?
    a) Have you found a way to let your partner know what makes you feel uncomfortable?
    b) If so, are you satisfied with the way the two of you have dealt with it?

Intimacy and Holiness

Judaism has always taught that true intimacy is holy. To draw near and cleave to another, to truly trust and love another, is holy. In fact, we are taught that our intimate human relationships are a model for the type of relationship we can have with God, as individuals and as part of the Jewish people. We treat those relationships and things that embody holiness in ways that are distinctive, in ways that set them apart.

Our masters taught: He who loves his wife as his own person, who honors her more than his own person . . . of him, Scripture says, "And you shall know that your tent is in peace" (Job 5:24).

BT *Y'vamot* 62b

A Jewish wedding is a time for two people to publicly affirm that they treat each other as they treat no others, that they set each other apart as holy and precious. In fact, the Hebrew word for wedding, *kiddushin*, is related to the Hebrew word *kadosh*, "holy." Both come from the root meaning to set apart, to make distinct. As you move toward your wedding day, consider the ways in which you have seen others set each other apart and treat each other as they do no one else, and consider the ways that you have already begun to do that with each other.

Exercise 11. Models of Holy Relationships

Part I

Separately, prepare lists of people whose marital relationships you consider to be models.

Part II

For each relationship you have listed, write down the positive characteristics you see in the relationship.

Part III

Think of specific actions or interactions you have witnessed in this couple that underscore those aspects of their relationship you would like to have in yours.

Part IV

Share your work with each other. Compare the characteristics you value. See if the same actions resonate similarly with both of you.

Exercise 12. *K'dushah* (Holiness) Time Line

Part I

Prepare a time line, beginning with the day you met. Place on the time line any interaction or moment that for you was a sign that you were setting your partner apart from all others, treating or perceiving him or her in a distinct manner. Also, place on your time line any interaction or moment that for you was a sign that your partner was setting you apart from all others, treating or perceiving you in a distinct manner. These can be large things, like moving in together, going on a vacation together, or introducing you to family members, or they can be smaller things, like modifying a schedule to attend something that meant a great deal to you or shopping and picking up your favorite chocolate. Think broadly.

Part II

Share your time lines with each other and discuss their contents. Take time to ponder those moments that were significant for one of you that the other had not taken note of or had forgotten.

⚜ Conditions and Promises: Intimacy ⚜

Together, articulate a few statements about the ways in which you will try to maintain intimacy and preserve sh'lom bayit.

Taharat HaMishpachah: *A Perspective from Tradition*

Traditionally, the Jewish legal system established boundaries for sexual intimacy, known as family purity laws, in Hebrew, *taharat hamishpachah*. While these laws may seem archaic today, it is still possible to learn something from the understanding of relationships that lies behind the details of the laws themselves. Central to this complex system about sexual permissibility is the notion that a woman's menstrual flow precludes physical contact with her husband. Therefore, for the week of her flow and the week following, they cannot have any physical contact. Then, before they reestablish sexual contact, she must immerse herself in a *mikveh*, a ritual bath. In practice, in traditional Jewish communities, this means a married couple is only permitted to have sex two weeks out of the month.

According to Blu Greenberg, a contemporary Orthodox Jewish writer:

> *Taharat HaMishpachah* implies that sex is a special part of marriage, but only a part. Early on, one learns that sex is not all there is to love, that not every newlywed spat can be settled in bed, that for almost half the month *niddah* [the period when the couple cannot have sex] requires of us to develop other, more difficult, more sophisticated modes of communication.
>
> Blu Greenberg,
> *How to Run a Traditional Jewish Household*
> (New York: Simon and Schuster, 1983)

Family purity laws have not been regularly practiced among liberal Jews for quite some time, because they seem to stigmatize menstruation and inhibit spontaneous sexual expression. Nonetheless, some couples have chosen to practice these laws in order to give some rhythm and balance to their sex lives. While observing these stringent laws may hold little or no interest for you, perhaps you and your partner might consider specific ways to remind yourselves of the sanctity of sex. Remember: Judaism teaches that all aspects of life—including sex—can reflect our understanding of and commitment to holiness.

4

Family, Friends, and Free Time

Your Family

Hence, a man leaves his father and mother and clings to his wife, so that they become one flesh.

Genesis 2:24

Until you are married, you are officially members of different families. You have no recognized links to each other's parents, siblings, or grandparents and, therefore, no responsibilities toward them. Conversely, they have no connections with you and no responsibilities toward you. When you publicly affirm your connection to each other, when you say that your primary family obligation will be to the new family that the two of you are forming, all of that will change. You will each have a family-in-law, and your families of origin will have new extended members as well. You will have enduring relationships with family members who are already deceased as well as ties to the family members who are yet to be in your new spouse's family. Families are multigenerational; people become members through birth, adoption, and marriage, and they never fully leave the emotional life of a family, even after death or divorce. Families have a life of memories and hopes that each of you is agreeing to take on as your own through this marriage.

During the weeks, months, or years that you have known each other, you have come to know various members of each other's families. Your first impressions were probably colored by the information you were given by your partner about each member. However, in time, you have not only developed your own impressions and understandings of these people, who are soon to be members of your family, but you have also created your own independent relationships with them. These evolving relationships are sure to continue to change and develop as you all go through different life transitions. As a new family in formation, you may benefit from reflecting upon the patterns you have established to this point and the patterns you establish as you plan for your wedding. Identifying ways in which you would like to invest in and further develop certain aspects of your relationships can help you deepen existing ties. Moreover, if you see already established patterns that bother or worry you or that you know you would not like to continue over the years, now is the time to consider how much harder it can be to break a pattern than to begin one.

Becoming Family to Each Other's Family

Some families excel at incorporating new members. They naturally reach out and embrace newcomers as their own. Other families have closed or semi-closed boundaries. They may be cordial and even include someone new in family activities; however, when they identify family members, it is ultimately only blood relatives who count. In some families, such distinctions are overt and ever present. In other families, it can be quite subtle and less discernible to those not directly affected.

Jessica and Larry had known each other since they were in high school. Nine years later, they were talking seriously about marriage. As kids, Larry met Jessica's parents when he went to her house after school or to pick her up for a date. Jessica's parents had always been nice to him, inviting him to stay for dinner, and asking interested questions about things going on in his life. Jessica's parents had met when they were fairly young and understood that anyone Jessica met along the way could be their future son-in-law. Larry's parents, on the other hand, had infrequent and brief interactions with Jessica. They were less interested in getting to know her, figuring Larry and Jessica were very young and, if and when things got serious, there would be plenty of time to get to know her. They themselves had each dated many people and had been involved in long-term, serious relationships before they met each other. They felt that if they expressed any clear interest in

Jessica, it would be perceived as pressure. But because their approach was so different from that of her own parents, Jessica had the impression that they did not particularly like her and that they hoped Larry would meet someone else. When she occasionally mentioned her understanding of the situation to Larry, he would dismiss it as overly sensitive and an unfair read of his parents.

Brian felt his parents never gave him the time he wanted to get to know someone on his own terms, as an independent being. From as early as he could remember, his parents would ask him endless questions, often personal and embarrassing questions, about the girls he spoke to on the phone or took out. He often felt badgered into inviting someone to come to dinner with his parents. When he went off to college, he never mentioned anyone to them. As far as they knew, he had no social life at all. After being involved with Susan for almost a year, he mentioned her to his parents and told them that she would be coming to visit for a week during the summer. When Susan arrived, they were cordial but cool. Because they hadn't heard anything about Susan prior to Brian's mentioning that she would come for a visit, they assumed the two were just friends. As they watched Brian and Susan interact, it became clear that they were involved with each other. Brian's mother was furious—Brian had kept them in the dark, Brian did not trust them. Or, worse, Brian's relationship with them had changed because of Susan. Susan had to be the one behind this. It had to be Susan's fault that Brian's behavior and communication with his parents had shifted.

Each of us goes through significant transitions as we enter the world of dating, become aware of our sexual feelings, and struggle to understand the impact that our words and actions have upon other people. But it is also important to realize that a young person's coming of age, testing the waters of intimate and personal relationships, is equally confusing and unfamiliar to his or her parents. No one has a road map for this period of life. Generally, parents have two things to turn to: their own personal experiences and memories, and the experiences of peers who have older children. In many ways, Jessica's and Larry's parents relied heavily on their own personal experiences as they attempted to act appropriately when their children began to date. Brian's parents, whose own parents had never shown any interest in their personal lives, had promised themselves that they would let their children know they were interested and cared and could be trusted with confidences.

**Exercise 13. Parental Interest and Involvement:
A Multigenerational Affair**

Together, discuss the following questions:

1. How long did your parents know each other before they became engaged?
2. What messages did your parents give you, directly or indirectly, about dating and making commitments?
3. How accepting were your grandparents of their children-in-law?
4. How accepting have your parents been of the person you love?
5. Do you see any discernible patterns from one generation to the next?

The first time Emily visited Steven's parents' house she immediately felt at home. His parents were warm and welcoming. They were interested in many of the same things she was, and conversation was both entertaining and challenging. She was able to relax and enjoy their company. They were respectful of the time and space alone that Emily and Steven wanted to have, even encouraging them to go out on one of the nights that Emily and Steven had assumed they would all spend together. Subsequent visits proved to be the same, as did her interactions with other members of Steven's family when she met them. Emily and Stephen were delighted to find they were accepted as a couple and as individuals and that they could comfortably express themselves with all of the members of Steven's family.

Stephanie was struck by Bob's mother's generosity when she came as a visitor to her home. She had cooked a lavish meal and was very interested in Stephanie. But Stephanie began to feel uncomfortable as the months and years passed. Visits were always the same—she was a guest in Bob's mother's home. They talked about current events and Bob's cousins and aunts and uncles, many of whom Stephanie did not know personally. And they never talked about anything of substance. Stephanie was shocked when her future mother-in-law invited her to call her mom. She had felt like she had been kept at arm's length. Moreover, when Bob's mother introduced her to friends, she displayed a closeness and overt affection toward Stephanie that seemed all for show. For Bob's mother, she was Bob's wife-to-be, not a family member, not a person in her own right. During the engagement, close family friends of Bob's mother invited her and her children to come for a holiday dinner. Without thinking twice, Bob's mother called him with the invitation, but as he had to work that night, he declined. No invitation was offered to Stephanie. When confronted afterward, without blinking an eye, Bob's mother said to him, "She invited our family. You should have told me Stephanie wanted to come. I assumed she wouldn't." Stephanie's perceptions were confirmed. Her future mother-in-law still did not think of her as a member of the family. She was someone who simply came along with Bob to family gatherings.

Exercise 14. Open and Closed Families

Family counselors use a graphic tool, known as a genogram, to depict multiple generations in a family and to indicate degrees of closeness and distance. Through the genogram, individuals can gain an understanding about relationship patterns within their families of origin and within the families they create.

Part I

Separately, with the information you have, generate genograms for your own family and for your partner's family.

Part II

Compare your genograms and discuss what you have learned.

> ### Part III
>
> *If you have encountered information or patterns that you would like to pursue further, consider engaging a mental health professional to guide you through the process.*
>
> *For more information on genograms, see Genograms: Assessment and Intervention by Monica McGoldrick (NY: W. W. Norton, 1999), or go to: northwestern.edu/commstud/galvin/genograms*

How to Deal with Serious Rejection

Our masters taught: A little boy may be trusted if he says, My daddy told me that his family is fit [to marry into priestly families], while that family is unfit, and we ate at the *Ketzatzah* [the cutting off] when the daughter of So-and-so was married to So-and-so.

What is *Ketzatzah?* If one of several brothers has wed a wife who is not fit for him, the other members of his family come around and bring a jar full of parched corn and nuts, and in the presence of the children break it in the open space [before the house], saying, "Our brethren of the House of Israel, hear! Our brother So-and-so has wed a wife who is not fit for him, and we fear that his issue will commingle with our issue. Come and take some of these as a token for future generations, so that his issue will not commingle with our issue." The children pick up [what has been scattered], saying, "So-and-so has been cut off from his family." Should the brother divorce such a wife, his family would perform the same ceremony, saying, "So-and-so has returned to his family."

BT *K'tubot* 28b; JT *Kiddushin* 1:5

Thank goodness some of our people's folk practices have ceased to exist! A family's having license to make a public spectacle of their dissatisfaction with a child's mate was once socially condoned. In most communities, it no longer is. Instead, discomfort with and refusal to accept a child's mate are now largely private affairs. The reactions, though, are no less hurtful.

Six years after Jason and Barbara married, Jason's father called their home. Barbara answered the phone and asked her father-in-law how he was doing. He said, "Fine. And how are Jason's children?" This was not a man with a sense of humor. He had never liked Barbara, never reached out to her. However, he was delighted to have grandchildren. They were an extension of *his* family, through *his* son Jason. For him, they were Jason's children. Fortunately, for Jason and Barbara, their sense of themselves as a family was not dependent on their interactions with Jason's father. While the wound never fully healed, Barbara was able to experience the love, acceptance, and support that Jason, the rest of his extended family, her family, and their friends constantly offered.

Exercise 15. Dealing with Family Responses

Part I

Separately, prepare lists of the following:

1. The ways in which members of your partner's family of origin have expressed their feelings that you will become a member of their family.
2. The ways in which members of your family of origin have expressed their feelings about your choice of a spouse.

Part II

Separately, write something about the following:

1. Your initial responses to your family's responses to your chosen mate.
2. Your subsequent responses to their expressed dissatisfaction.
3. Your initial responses to your mate's family's responses to you.
4. Your subsequent responses to their expressed dissatisfaction.

Part III

Share and discuss with your partner your responses to parts 1 and 2.

Part IV

Discuss with each other your level of comfort and satisfaction with your responses as individuals and as a couple to negative interactions with family members. Brainstorm with each other about ways to deal with hostile family members.

Dealing with rejection or indifference from members of your partner's family or expressed by your family toward your partner can be exceedingly painful and confusing. It can put stress on your relationship, as you anticipate interactions, experience them, and process them afterward. Remembering that while these are people with whom you will be interacting for many years to come, they are not the only people upon whom your sense of self depends. In addition to being supports for each other, let others be there for you as well.

Family Gatherings

For many adults, negotiating comfortable means of interacting with parents and other relatives as an independent adult was a struggle. As the two of you become a family unit, you will have two families with whom you must negotiate. While you were single, you and your families figured out your own way to deal with your vacation time, holiday celebrations, and family occasions. Now, as a unit, you will have to figure out all of this again, because you have two families to consider. Perhaps, if you have known each other a long time, you have worked all of this out. For many of you, these are either yet unresolved issues or issues that you have tried to respond to in a variety of ways, without deciding upon a single pattern.

Dan and Shoshanah had found their first Thanksgiving and Passover easy. They packed their bags, and each went home to their own parents' houses. Each of their families had elaborate, extended family gatherings, and neither one of them could imagine missing out on the festivities they had always known and enjoyed. Now that they were engaged though, the two families extended invitations early, vying for the couple to spend the holiday with them. Shoshanah saw no reason to schlep to her future in-laws' house when she would much prefer to be with her family. Dan wanted them to spend the holidays together and to choose one place or the other. They went back and forth, neither one convincing the other that there was a clear and compelling reason for them to give up their preference. In each case, spending the holiday meant more than just an evening's meal. Both families lived out of town and it meant spending three to five days. They agreed it would be easier to split for the holidays; the largest number of people would be satisfied and able to spend the holidays in the ways they were most comfortable. Dan and Shoshanah recognized that this solution would only work until they had children. Then, another set of discussions and decisions would have to be made.

Terry and Jon had met in college. Jon's family lived nearby, and the two of them had spent Thanksgiving with Jon's family throughout their years in college. Once they graduated and moved to another state, battles ensued with both Jon's and Terry's families. Terry's family felt they had been very generous not to argue with Terry when he said he wanted to go home with Jon for Thanksgiving. Jon's family was local; they weren't. It made sense. But now they weren't near either family. It was Terry's family's turn to have them come to their house. Jon's family, on the other hand, had assumed Jon and Terry had made a commitment to spend Thanksgiving with them in perpetuity. They were terribly hurt that the two of them were considering an alternative to what they had thought was an established holiday tradition. Jon and Terry were torn.

Will any of these approaches work for you? How can you negotiate your own solutions?

In-Laws

When the kid and the leopard dwell together, daughter-in-law and mother-in-law will dwell together.

Chuppat Eliyahu

Honor your father-in-law and mother-in-law because henceforth they are your parents.

Tobit 10:12

There is nothing simple or predictable about the ways in-laws relate to each other! The English language and Anglo-Saxon social structure provide an interesting construct to understand the relationship established among families following a marriage. A person does not become a brother or a mother, but a brother-in-law or a mother-in-law. There is no linguistic assumption of affection or emotional connections, merely a legal tie. In fact, as emotional bonds develop, many people feel that describing someone as an in-law falls short, because of its sterility and associations with distance and struggle.

In your relationship, you have referred to each other in different ways in public and in private. In addition to first names and perhaps nicknames, you may have referred to each other as "the person I'm dating," the "person I'm seeing," my "boyfriend/my girlfriend," and "my fiancé/e." And in the future, you will use terms such as "my wife," "my husband," and "my life partner."

Naming Your Future In-Laws

When Alyssa first met her in-laws, she referred to them as Mr. and Mrs. Buchsbaum. This seemed to be comfortable for everyone. As she began to feel closer to them, she wanted to drop the formality. But she was hesitant about asking them if it would be all right to call them by their first names. She felt that the invitation should come from them, from their desire to acknowledge a different level of relationship. For a while, she dropped the "Mr." and "Mrs." and didn't address them directly at all. If she wanted to start a conversation, she would catch their eye and jump right in. If she was speaking to one about the other, she would say, "I was talking with your wife/husband and. . . ." This was not a great solution, but it was better than using titles. She hoped that after the wedding they would ask her to call them something less formal.

When Henry met Lauren's parents they immediately invited him to use their first names. He tried to comply with their wishes, but every so often he would call one of them Mr. or Mrs. Hirschfeld. When he did, they would give him a disappointed look and remind him that he didn't need to be so formal with them. When Henry and Lauren announced their engagement, Lauren's parents began to refer to him as their son, and they asked him to call them mom and dad. They said it was their way of showing him how thrilled they were that he was becoming an official member of the family. They already loved him and felt so close to him. Henry felt the same way toward them. But, "mom" and "dad" were names reserved for his own parents, and using them for anyone else felt strange. He didn't want to hurt Lauren's parents, but he couldn't call them mom and dad.

Exercise 16. Future Parents-in-Law

Part I

Separately, write down your answers to the following:

1. How do you believe your future in-laws would like you to address them?
2. How have they communicated this to you?
3. How comfortable do you feel with the current situation?
4. Do you think they will want you to call them something else in the future?
5. What would you like to call them?
6. Who do you believe should initiate a name change?
7. How do you believe a potential name change ought to be negotiated?
8. How comfortable are you with the way you and your partner have handled this? If you are not comfortable, how would you like it to be different?

Part II

Share your responses with your partner.

Part III

Separately, answer the following questions:

1. How do your future in-laws refer to you to family and friends?
2. Are you comfortable with this?
   a) If not, have you, individually or collectively, let them know?
   b.) How did they respond?
3. Do you anticipate changes in the way they refer to you in the future?
4. What would be your preference?
5. How can you let them know this?

Part IV

Discuss your responses with your partner.

Siblings-in-Law

> Rava said: He who is about to take a wife should inquire about her brothers, as intimated in Scripture's saying, Aaron took Elisheba, the daughter of Amminadab, the sister of Nahshon [Exodus 6:23]. Since she is spoken of as the daughter of Amminadab, is it not obvious that she is also the sister of Nahshon? Why, then, is it added that she was also the sister of Nahshon? To intimate that when a man takes a wife, he should inquire about [the character] of her brothers.
>
> BT *Bava Batra* 110a

Each of you comes to the other's family already having had an array of experiences with your own siblings, aunts, and uncles and with your parents as they interacted with their siblings-in-law. As you start to look at each other's siblings as future members of your own family, you bring these experiences with you in the form of hopes, expectations, and concerns. You may seek to replicate or avoid the type of relationships you have had with your own siblings or that your parents had with theirs. You may hope to find a closeness with your siblings-in-law that you have not experienced with your own siblings. You may have wonderful models from your parents' relationships with each other's siblings that lead you to seek the same for yourself, or you may have models that lead you to have little or no expectations at all. Furthermore, depending on your relationships and perceptions of your aunts and uncles and the roles they have played in your lives, you may find yourself looking at your partner's siblings not only as your peers, but as the future aunts and uncles of your own children. Getting a sense of how your experiences are influencing your expectations in this area can be a help to you, in both the long and short run.

Amelia disliked Rick's brother from the day she met him. Corey was loud and crude, his humor was raunchy, and he never seemed to have a kind word to say about anything or anyone. When he and Rick were together, Rick acted like a sixteen-year-old. Amelia had let Rick know how uncomfortable she was with Corey, and Rick had dismissed it, saying that they rarely saw him. Amelia's concerns only grew as her relationship with Rick deepened. How would she feel having Corey at every family celebration? How would she feel having him as her children's uncle? Ideally, she imagined her children knowing and loving their aunts and uncles. But what sorts of things would he introduce them to, and what kind of role model would he be?

Tom's sister was not like anyone else Melissa had ever met. She was exceedingly bright and well read. Yet, she had chosen not to get a college education and instead had developed her skills as a weaver. She lived in a small community of artists and showed her weavings at craft fairs around the country and around the world. Melissa fantasized about the things she could learn from her future sister-in-law and the world of options that her children would be exposed to because of her.

From the day they met, Lisa and Miriam felt they understood each other. When Lisa and Todd were with Todd's extended family, Lisa and Miriam would sit for hours talking about everything under the sun. Miriam was creative and warm and curious. Lisa so looked forward to having Miriam as a sister-in-law. Her mother had never been close to Lisa's aunt, her father's sister. So, as far as Lisa was concerned, this was a delightful and unexpected bonus of her love for Todd.

Exercise 17. Siblings-in-Law

Part I. Models and Expectations

Separately, answer the following questions and then discuss together:

1. How close were your parents to their brothers- and sisters-in-law?
2. How did their relationships evolve?
3. Do you expect to have similar relationships with your siblings-in-law?

Part II. Current Sibling-in-Law Relationships

Discuss the following questions:

1. How well do you know your future siblings-in-law?
2. What factors have contributed to your current relationships?
3. Are you satisfied with your current relationships?
4. What fantasies do you have about what your relationships with siblings-in-law might be?
5. Is it plausible to try to transform your fantasies into reality?

❧ Conditions and Promises: Family ☙

Talk with each other about the conditions you feel comfortable establishing with each other regarding your interactions with each other's family members. Discuss how they relate to your sense of being ready or willing to make a long-term commitment to each other.

Try to articulate the promises you want to make as a new family regarding your extended family. Write down those things that you can agree upon.

Those No Longer Here and Those Not Yet Born

It may seem strange, at this point in your relationship, to have a focused discussion about the generations who preceded you and those you anticipate in your future. But, in reality, your family is a link in a chain that started long before you were born and will continue long after you die. Family members who are no longer present, due to death, divorce, or estrangement, continue to influence the dynamics of your family. Each of you is also influenced by your expectations about having or raising children within your new family. Therefore, you can gain clarity about the family you hope to establish if you take time now to acknowledge the power that past and future generations have on your current plans.

Those No Longer Here

Lee was forever surprised by the frequency with which Sam and his family referred to Sam's grandfather. Though he had died more than fifteen years earlier, he was still ever present. At every family celebration, at the ballpark, at synagogue. Anything at all could trigger a smile, a tear, or a memory of him. Lee felt that in many ways she knew Sam's grandfather, though they had clearly never met. She wished that she had known him; it sounded as if he was a wonderful, loving man. Lee hoped that their children would have as memorable and profound a relationship with one of their older relatives as Sam had shared with his grandfather.

When Bill and Joan attended the *b'rit milah* for Bill's nephew, Joan was surprised that so little was shared about Richard, the baby's namesake. She knew that Richard had been Bill's father's brother. She knew that he had died as a young adult and that, prior to his death, Bill's father and Richard had been very close. Thirty-five years had passed, but as Bill told Joan, Richard's name only came up when old family albums were taken out and, then, his father always absented himself. Bill himself knew very little about Richard. But both Bill and his brother knew that it was customary to name a child for a deceased relative. They only hoped for this newborn boy what they had been able to glean from pictures, that he would have a happy childhood and that he would be close with his siblings.

Abby and Liz had been together for six years. They had long ago met many of each other's family members. They spent long weekends with Abby's extended family—multiple generations of aunts, uncles, and cousins. Abby was stunned when, one day, Liz hung up the phone from speaking with her mother and was on the verge of tears. Liz's mother had just told her that, Betty, a woman who had been like an aunt to Liz when she was a young child, had died. Abby asked Liz when she had last seen her. Tears welled up in Liz's eyes. She couldn't remember the last time. Betty had been a constant presence from the time Liz had been three or four until she was about nine years old. She loved it when she came home from school and found Betty at the house or when she and her family went to Betty's house. Betty had a way of making her feel wonderful and special. But her mom had had a falling out with Betty. While Betty had disappeared from Liz's life, the memory of Betty's love and presence never did.

Exercise 18. Those No Longer Here

Part I

Separately, write the following lists:

1. People who have died who left an indelible impression on you.
2. People your partner has told you about who have died and left an indelible impression on him or her.

Part II

Share your lists with each other. Fill each other in on people who are not well known.

Part III

Share with each other what responsibilities you feel to those people who are no longer here.

Part IV

Write a list of people who were once central in your life or your family's life with whom you no longer have contact or have minimal contact.

Part V

Share the following with your partner:

1. What life was like, from your perspective, when each of these people was more of a constant presence.
2. The conclusions you reached as a result of the changed nature of your relationship with these people.

Those Not Yet Born: Expectations

For most of human history, marriage was equated with having children. There was an expectation that within a year or two of marriage, the first child would come into the family and others would follow soon thereafter. These expectations were often fulfilled because of the proscribed role women played in the larger society and because of the ineffective means available for birth control and family planning.

Today, as you look toward your future, there are many more possibilities open to you. You can choose whether or not you want to have children, when you want to have them, and how many you would like to have. Numerous options for birth control and family planning are available, along with a wide range of possibilities for creating families through adoption, artificial insemination, and genetic engineering that far exceed even the wildest imaginings of former generations. While today's circumstances may seem ideal, the truth is they also introduce variables that necessitate serious discussions and decision making.

Zach and Nina had discussed having kids. They both had grown up expecting to marry and have children. As they spoke with some friends one night, they were stunned by the course of the conversation. One of their friends asked them if they planned to have kids after they married. Without skipping a beat, they both said, "Yes." The friend then asked them how many kids. Zach said, "I don't know. Two, maybe three." Nina said, "Really? I was thinking of having just one. It's really expensive to raise kids these days." Zach said, "We'll see." Nina nodded. She trusted they would work it out. The friend then asked, "How soon after you marry do you plan to have kids?" Zach said, "I don't know. Probably seven to ten years from now. I want us to be settled, maybe in a home of our own." Nina shook her head in disagreement, with a small, sad smile on her face. Clearly they had more talking to do.

Neil and Pam agreed—they were a two-career family and they would always be a two-career family. They both loved the careers they had chosen and the fulfillment they got from their jobs. They also loved the lifestyle they had as a result of the money they both brought in. They had discussed having children a number of times. They agreed that they would not want to have children who were raised by a nanny. Neither of them was willing to commit to having a reduced workload, and neither thought it fair to expect the other to do so either. Yet, both saw themselves becoming parents some time in the future.

Exercise 19. Preliminary Thoughts on Having Children

Part I

Separately, write down the following:

1. Your expectations for yourself regarding parenthood: as a child, as an adolescent, as a young adult, now.
2. What influenced your expectations at each stage?

Part II

Share your list with your partner. See if you are currently in the same place.

Part III

Separately, answer the following questions:

1. If you do want to have children, how many would you like to have? Why?
2. How much time would you like to wait between children?
3. How soon would you like to start to add children to your family? Why?

Part IV

Share your responses with your partner.

Part V

Discuss with each other the differences in your answers.

Parental Responsibilities: Models and Expectations

The Sages said in the name of Rabbi Yosei bar Chanina: In Usha, an ordinance was enacted that a man is required to maintain his sons and daughters while they are small.

BT *K'tubot* 50a

Rabbi Eleazar said: A father must hold himself responsible for his son until the age of thirteen. After that, he should say, Blessed be God who has freed me of liabilty for this boy.

B'reishit Rabbah 63:10

. . . a father is obligated to circumcise him, to redeem him [if he is the firstborn], to teach him Torah, to teach him a craft, and to get him married. Some say: Also to teach him how to swim.

BT *B'rachot* 7b

Definitions of good parenting have changed significantly over time. In fact, our understanding of the child-parent relationship is ever evolving. Your grandparents probably utilized both inherited methods of child rearing and the advice of their generation's experts. The same can probably be said for your parents. Each had successes and failures; each learned along the way. In all likelihood, your parents did not see eye to eye on every matter related to child rearing. And even more likely, the two of you had very different experiences as children regarding limit setting, expectations, and communication.

Rav Huna, in the name of Rabbi Yochanan, told the parable of a certain man who opened a perfume shop for his son in the street of harlots. The street plied its trade, the perfume business plied its trade, and the lad, like any young male, plied his natural inclination—he strayed into depraved ways. When the father came and caught him with a harlot, he began to shout, "I'll kill you!" But the father's friend was there, and he spoke up. "You yourself ruined your son, and now you are yelling at him! You ignored all other occupations and taught him to be a perfumer; you ignored all other streets and deliberately opened a shop for him on the street of harlots!"

Sh'mot Rabbah 43:7

It happened in Lod that when a son of Gorgos ran away from school, the father threatened to box his ears. The son, terrorized by his father, went off and drowned himself in a cistern.

S'machot 2:4–5

Now, as you contemplate the possibility of the two of you not only sharing your lives together, but sharing responsibilities as parents for your children, consider what you have experienced and what you have learned, as well as your hopes and expectations.

Alexis thought Kate's parents overindulged their children. As she listened to Kate talk about her childhood, she was appalled at the amount of toys and the types of trips her parents had given her. She never had to work until she was done with college. She merely had to say " please" and "thank you" and everything she expressed an interest in or desire for her parents provided. Alexis, on the other hand, had never felt deprived in any way. But she had been given a small allowance for the things she did around the house and understood, from the time she was in her teens, that any additional money she might want she would have to earn on her own. From the time she was fourteen, she had always had a job. First baby-sitting, then working at a local camp, then at a restaurant, then a bookstore. Her parents paid for her education and basic living expenses; she paid for everything else.

Exercise 20. Models and Expectations of Parental Responsibilities

Part I

Separately, prepare lists of the following:

1. The responsibilities you feel your parents took on for you.
2. The responsibilities you believe your partner's parents took on for him/her.

Part II

Share with your partner how you feel about the following:

1. The way things worked in your parents' house(s).
2. What you know about how things worked in your partner's home(s).

Exercise 21. The Responsiblities You Will Share

Part I

Separately, prepare lists of the following:

1. The responsibilities you feel you will have to your children (e.g., general education, religious education, skills, attitudes, values).
2. What you would like to provide for your children.
3. What you consider reasonable expectations for a five-year-old, a ten-year-old, a fifteen-year-old, a twenty-two-year-old, a twenty-eight-year-old.
4. Characteristics you associate with overindulgent or withholding parents.

Part II

Share your lists and examples with each other. Discuss any discrepancies.

Part III

Consider how you will negotiate the differences in your perceptions and expectations.

Exercise 22. Being an Example: Looking Back and Looking Forward

Part I

Separately, answer the following:

1. What kind of role models were your parents?
2. What positive things did you learn from your parents' example? What negative?
3. What were your parents' inconsistencies?
4. What would you like to model for your children?
5. What do you hope your partner will model for your children?

Part II

Share your lists with each other and discuss them.

Part III

Discuss how you can work together to raise the type of children you want to have.

〜 Conditions and Promises: Parenthood 〜

Discuss the expectations you hold for the children you might raise and the expectations you have for yourselves as you raise them.

Try to articulate specific things you will try to help each other uphold with regard to your future interactions with and messages conveyed to your children.

Genetic Disorders, Sexually Transmitted Diseases, and Fertility

It seemed that from the time that Gene and Maggie met they were fantasizing about the children they would have. "They'll have your blue eyes." "And they'll have your athletic prowess." "They'll have your sense of direction." "And your way with people." They spoke endlessly about what they looked forward to doing with their kids. For each of them, having and raising children were an essential part of what it meant to be married, what it meant to be fully adult. Never did it occur to them that they could encounter obstacles to having children of their own.

Facing the Future with Realistic Optimism

As you discuss your future plans, if children are part of the picture, you can use the period of your engagement to gain some realistic information about your own health and the viability of your dreams about becoming parents.

If the two of you are Jewish, particularly both of Ashkenazi or both of Sephardi extraction, you should seriously consider genetic testing. Geneticists have found that because of the inbreeding among Jews for many centuries, certain genetic mutations and anomalies have been passed down. Some of these genetic predispositions do not manifest themselves with any predictability. Yet, if both parents are carriers, some genetic disorders can be passed to offspring, with devastating results.

If the two of you have been sexually active teens and adults, perhaps you have already been tested for sexually transmitted diseases. If you have not been tested in the last six months, consider getting tested again. Liberal Judaism advises sexually active adults who have not been monogamous since last being tested to get retested. This way, sexual partners can interact with each other openly and honestly, the infected partner can receive treatment in a timely fashion, with hopes of arresting or eradicating the disease, and if the disease can affect fertility, appropriate testing and counseling can be sought.

If either one or both of you have reason to be concerned about the possibility of infertility, due to a family history or your personal health history, there are some tests you can have done now. Some couples feel that they want to make their final decision about marriage with full knowledge. Others feel that this knowledge will not make or break their personal commitment to each other. They decide that if, God forbid, they are faced with fertility problems, they will then explore all of the options available to them.

The Torah is filled with stories of couples who longed to have children of their own but were unable to do so. Even the great love story of Jacob and Rachel speaks of the confusion and desperation of a couple unable to conceive or bear children. For years, every other woman in Jacob's household, Leah and the two handmaidens Bilhah and Zilpah, were able to have children. Rachel, though, bore none. Finally, one day she said to her beloved husband, Jacob, "Give me children, or else I am dead" (Genesis 30:1). Her sense of meaning and self-worth were tied to her dream, her need to become a parent.

Exercise 23. Dreams and Self-Expectations

Discuss the following questions with your partner:

1. How is your image of yourself as an adult tied to becoming a parent?
2. Is your sense of becoming a parent tied to your image of yourself as a sexual being? To being male or female?
3. Do you believe that you have an obligation to have children? What is the source of your sense of obligation?

Options and Alternatives

Infertility is the common plight of the biblical Matriarchs and Patriarchs. In addition to Jacob and Rachel, Abraham and Sarah, and Isaac and

Rebekah, also had their dreams of having and raising children thwarted or deferred. Sarah decided to give her handmaiden Hagar to Abraham as her surrogate. Rachel brought mandrakes, a folk aphrodisiac, to her husband in the hopes that they would lead to a viable conception.

Liberal Judaism encourages those who wish to have children to seek out ways to fulfill those hopes. However, this encouragement comes with a caveat. Having children should be exciting and exhilarating. It should bring a couple closer together, not drive them apart or produce unnecessary strains upon their relationship.

Fertility Treatments

Ray and Samantha wished it were as simple as finding some mandrakes. They had now spent five years and more money than they cared to count attempting to conceive. They'd gone from specialist to specialist being tested. Then they followed her ovulation cycle. She took pills. He got shots. Nothing seemed to help. They considered having Samantha go on the fertility drugs that often result in multiple births. But neither of them was particularly comfortable with that as an alternative. Why was something that was supposed to happen naturally proving to be so complicated?

Adoption

> He who brings up a child is called father, not he who merely begot him.
>
> *Sh'mot Rabbah* 46:5

Janet and Rhonda knew that they could never produce a child of their own. They also knew that they wanted to be parents. Rhonda's closest friend, who herself had been adopted, had recently met her birth mother and learned about her mother's circumstances at the time of her birth. She, her birth mother, and her adopted parents all agreed that her life was far better for having been adopted. Janet and Rhonda agreed that they would adopt two or three children.

Surrogacy

Cara and Evan had gone through all sorts of tests and learned that the seizures Cara was having during her pregnancy not only had caused the miscarriage, but could have been life-threatening for her. And so they explored their options. It was not a matter of either one or both of them being infertile. It was a matter of Cara not being able to carry to term. While they felt awkward at first, and though some members of their family objected on moral grounds, they found a woman to be a surrogate, so they could have a child to whom both of them were genetically linked.

Artificial Insemination and Genetic Engineering

> A woman who eats meat and drinks wine [during her pregnancy] will have healthy children. One who eats eggs will bear children with large eyes. One who eats fish will have charming children. One who eats parsley will have exceptionally handsome children. One who eats coriander will have fleshy children. One who eats etrog will have fragrant children.
>
> BT *K'tubot* 60b–61a

While our forebears may not have fully understood what influences the type of child someone has, they did recognize that some people would like to exert a large degree of control over the children they produce. Current technology allows for possibilities barely imagined by previous generations. For couples turning to donors, information is now available about the genetic characteristics and life achievements of prospective donors. In addition, tests such as amniocentesis allow prospective parents to weigh their options if congenital or genetic abnormalities are detected.

Joel and Arlene wanted to have daughters who would excel in the areas that they most valued. Neither one of them could imagine what their life or the life of their child would be like if she had a congenital disease or genetic disorder. They agreed that they would have Arlene tested when she became pregnant, to learn what they could about the child's genetic makeup. They agreed that if there were any genetic abnormalities, Arlene would abort.

Joanne and Glen wanted to have children, but Glen had had mumps as an adult and was incapable of having children of his own. They decided that the alternative they liked best was artificial insemination, since the baby would at least have a genetic link to Joanne. They learned about the different types of sperm banks that existed and checked them all out. When they found a place with which they were comfortable, they began looking at the descriptions of the donors. They wanted to find someone as close in looks, intelligence, and abilities to Glen as possible. They wanted their child and the people in the child's world to have as little reason to suspect that it was not Glen's child as possible.

Exercise 24. Should You Be Unable to Have Children of Your Own

Part I

Separately, rank in order your willingness to consider the following alternatives:

Adoption, artificial insemination, in vitro fertilization, surrogacy, fertility drugs.

Part II

Share your lists with each other. Share your responses to each other's lists. Explain your feelings and choices to each other.

Part III

Discuss how central you believe having/and or raising children is to your marital happiness.

✎ Conditions and Promises: Infertility ✎

Discuss with each other and write down any conditions or promises you would like to articulate now about the responses and support you would want if you find you are unable to conceive or bear children of your own.

Friends and Free Time

Marty and two of his best friends had had season tickets to the Celtics since they were in high school. All of them had remained in Boston during college and graduate school. They couldn't imagine anything that would put an end to their long-standing ritual. Cindy liked sports well enough, but more than a game or two a season was pushing it. She really liked Marty's high school buddies; they were great guys. At first, she was resentful those weeks when there was more than one game. She even joked with her girlfriends that she would have preferred someone who had one night a week out with the guys at a bar. But Cindy couldn't deny it: Marty always came home from the games relaxed and in a good mood. His buddies and the Celtics provided him with something that she couldn't.

Melinda spent at least an hour a night on the phone with friends. At first, Fred was jealous. He wanted to know what they talked about and why Melinda didn't just talk to him. He asked her to try talking to him instead of picking up the phone. After a few days, Melinda was irritable and Fred was confused. He was trying to pay close attention. He found most of what she talked about interesting. And when he didn't, he let her talk anyway. Melinda missed the give-and-take that her friends offered and the similar experiences that they drew on. She explained to Fred that she loved him dearly, but one of her girlfriends he would never be. At the same time, they would never be her husband, lover, and life partner.

Jeff loved to use his time away from work listening to music and reading books. Few things relaxed him in the same way. Jill liked to read but preferred to hike and get outside whenever she had a chance. They both wanted to spend more time together but resented compromising and having to spend some of their precious time off engaged in activities that they disliked. Eventually, they found ways to respect each other's preferences. They negotiated ways to be sure to be together, with friends or alone. It wasn't always easy, but they each felt that they weren't losing opportunities to do the things they enjoyed.

No two people are completely compatible and in sync 100 percent of the time. Every person's need for private time, quiet time, and social time is different. No two people can meet all of each other's needs.

Finding a comfortable way to enjoy friends and free time is important for the emotional and spiritual stability of your relationship. There are many, many possibilities. Each couple finds its own blend. And each couple has to regularly renegotiate the agreements they have made. You may make separate plans for weekday evenings and set weekends aside to be with each other. You may have a date night one weeknight and both weekend evenings, and leave the rest of the time for each of you to use as you desire. You may agree that there are certain friends you both enjoy spending time with and others you'd rather see alone. You may find that setting part of one weekend a month aside for your respective families works for you or that part of a vacation or holiday weekend is your best bet. Maybe vacations are a time to catch up with each other, with family, with friends, with books. Experimentation, communication, and negotiation will be the keys to your finding ways to meet your needs as individuals and as a couple.

Exercise 25. Friends and Free Time

Part I

Separately, write down a description of your ideal weeknight(s), your ideal weekend(s), and your ideal vacation.

Part II

Separately, write down a description of what you think your partner wrote down.

Part III

Decide which of you will go first. The first person shares his/her self-description with the other. Then, the other shares his/her guesses about his/her partner. No conversation is allowed. Listen, but don't argue or challenge.

Part IV

Discuss the differences and similarities.

Part V

Share with your partner what you learned about him/her through this exercise.

Part VI

Repeat parts 3 through 5 for the other partner.

Drugs and Alcohol

God, you formed the human body with infinite goodness. You have united in it innumerable forces incessantly at work like so many instruments, so as to preserve in its entirety this beautiful house containing one's immortal soul, and these forces act with all the order, concord, and harmony imaginable. If weakness or violent passion disturb this harmony, these forces act against one another. . . .

Moses Maimonides, *Physician's Prayer*

Karen had gotten used to Jeff's having a drink or two each night when he came home. It was part of his routine; he said it helped him relax and unwind. When they went to their first wedding together, Jeff and his buddies had a chugging contest. She'd never seen him drink like that before. Jeff assured her that he rarely drank excessively and that he was fine. When he went to get behind the wheel to drive them home, Karen refused to get in the car. Jeff was incensed. He was fine. They had a shouting match in the parking lot and went home separately. The next day, they had their first serious discussion about drugs and alcohol.

People's experiences with drugs and alcohol are as varied as the people themselves. Our relationships with alcohol and drugs are shaped by our families-of-origin, the eras in which we have lived, and the neighborhoods and communities among whom we have been socialized. Often, members of a couple find that they relate to drugs and alcohol in similar ways. However, drugs and alcohol can undermine a loving relationship. The quiz that follows is designed to help you articulate your attitudes toward drugs and alcohol, see how compatible your attitudes are, and determine if you, as individuals or as a couple, could benefit from some counseling. Do this exercise when you are both feeling comfortable and at ease with each other and more inclined to be open and non-defensive.

Exercise 26. Drugs and Alcohol

Part I

Separately, answer the following questions honestly:

1. Do you drink or use drugs more when you are disappointed, are under pressure, or have had a quarrel with someone?
2. Can you handle more drinks or drugs now than when you first started drinking or using?
3. Have you ever been unable to remember the previous evening or day, even though your friends say that you didn't pass out?
4. When drinking or using drugs with other people, do you try to have extra drinks or drugs when others won't know about it?
5. Do you sometimes feel uncomfortable if alcohol or drugs are not available?
6. Are you in more of a hurry to get your first drink or drug of the day than you used to be? (Do you have a first drink or drug of the day?)
7. Do you sometimes feel a little guilty about your drinking or drug use?
8. Has a family member or close friend ever expressed concern or complained about your drinking or drug use?
9. Do you often want to continue drinking or using drugs after your friends say they've had enough?
10. When you are sober, do you sometimes regret things you did or said while drinking or using drugs?
11. Have you ever had a DWI (driving while intoxicated) or DUI (driving under the influence of alcohol) violation or any other legal problem related to drinking or drugs?
12. Do you try to avoid family or close friends while you are drinking or using drugs?

13. What is your attitude toward the use of legal drugs, like alcohol, and illegal drugs like cocaine, marijuana, and heroin?

Part II

Based on your perception, answer these same questions about your partner.

Part III

Review your answers with your partner. Discuss any concerns or differences in perception you may have. If either of you feels that this is an area in which you can use professional help or peer support, seek it out.

Conditions and Promises: Free Time

Articulate your expectations and commitments regarding the use of your free time. Include any expectations or demands you may have regarding alcohol and drugs.

5

Names

Our God, God of our mothers
and our fathers! Sustain this child
through his/her parents' loving care.
Let him/her be known among our people
Israel by the name _____.
May his/her name be a source
of joy to us always. Inspire
him/her, O God, to serve our
people and all humankind.

Rabbi's Manual. Polish, David, ed.
(New York: CCAR Press, 1988)

When you were born, one of your parents' first official acts was to give you a name. If your family is of Eastern or Central European descent, you were probably named for a deceased relative. Among Ashkenazic Jews there was a long-standing belief that by giving a child such a name, parents were, in essence, giving the deceased person's soul to the child. For centuries, this folk practice held such power that many Ashkenazic Jews feared that conferring the name of living relatives was tantamount to robbing relatives of their souls. Among some communities, there was also a fear that if two people shared a name, they would share each other's fates. And certain communities went so far as to warn children from marrying into families in which a future parent-in-law shared their name.

Sometimes life experiences influenced the naming of a child: children born near Passover were sometimes called Pesach; children born to parents whose other children had suffered from illness and death sometimes called a child Alter (old) to give the power of long life to the child. Today, North American Jews of Ashkenazic descent often choose a name that shares a first letter with the name of the deceased person, rather than using the actual name. Others choose any English name they like, but give a Hebrew name that retains a connection with the person for whom the child is named.

These concerns were not shared by Jews in many other parts of the world. In fact, among Sephardic Jews, those who trace their lineage to pre-Inquisition Spain, naming a child for a living parent or close relative is a sign of great respect and love. In some Sephardic families, males are the third, fourth, even fifth in the family line to share a name.

Family names are a modern Jewish phenomenon. Jews took family names when the laws of the lands in which they lived required them to do so. The names they took often did more than identify the father. The most common sources for Jewish family names are the names of towns or regions from which they hailed, resulting, for example, in Moskowitz or Hamburger; the occupation in which the family engaged, such as Schneider, Yiddish for "tailor," or Handler, Yiddish for "merchant"; or the translation of the Hebrew "son of" into the vernacular, such as Abramson or Jacobson. Many Jews, when they arrived in America, changed their names or had them changed for them by immigration authorities. Some changed their names during the first decades that the family lived in America in an attempt to assimilate.

Share with each other what you know about your first and last names (English and, if you have one, Hebrew). If you don't know much about your names, talk with your parents and then with each other. If you don't have a Hebrew name, perhaps you might be interested in choosing one and taking it on prior to your wedding. Consider the ways in which Hebrew names have traditionally been chosen, and then speak with a rabbi about formalizing your selection.

The Power of Names

A good name is better than great riches.

Proverbs 22:1

In the Torah, and for most of Jewish life until the eighteenth century, Jews were simply known by their first name and then son/daughter of their father's first name, a name they kept for life (for example, Solomon son of David, or in Hebrew, Sholomo ben David). After marriage, a woman was also identified via her husband. She was known as the woman/wife of her husband. Rebekah, for example, was known as Rebekah wife of Isaac. Men, however, were never known as the husband or man of a particular woman.

The issue of what last name to take was not so simple for Laura and Ben. In fact, it almost ruined their wedding. Laura and Ben were both comfortable with Laura keeping her own name. However, two days before the wedding, they were thrown into a tailspin. Ben's father called Laura and told her that if she did not take his family name as her own, he would not be coming to the wedding. Stunned and angry, Laura told him that she hoped he would enjoy the pictures of the wedding.

Both reactions seem extreme. But the emotional pitch was so high because they both attached great significance to their family name. Ben's father had lost his entire family in the *Shoah* (Holocaust), and thus the survival of his name was even more crucial to him. He feared that if his son's family did not clearly bear his family name, it would soon be entirely lost. But Laura also had an emotional reason for wanting to keep her own name. Laura's father had died five years earlier, and she had a desire to retain her sense of connection with him. For her, keeping his name was a tangible way of doing so.

Ben and Laura's situation testifies to the power of names. Jewish tradition has always acknowledged this tremendous power. Names are never given, changed, or uttered lightly. The highest words of praise are "May his/her name be for a blessing." And the worst curse is "May his/her name be erased."

Even our Creation story highlights the power of names. One of Adam's first acts in the Garden of Eden was to name the animals:

> And God formed out of the earth all the wild beasts and all the birds of the sky, and brought them to Adam to see what he would call them; and whatever Adam called each living creature, that would be its name. And Adam gave names to all the cattle and to the birds of the sky and to all the wild beasts.
>
> Genesis 2:19–20

Choices and Decisions

Over the course of decades, each of us develops our own connections and associations with our family names. This is what makes the prospect of changing a name so emotionally charged. And since feminism began to question the value of a woman taking a man's last name, a custom whose origins go back to the notion of women being part of a man's property holdings, the choice of what name to take may be a political as well as a personal one.

For Francie Levine-Grater, choosing a name was most definitely a feminist issue. "The last name of a married woman," Franci said, "is a feminist marker." Franci's husband, however, felt strongly that they should have the same name. As Franci put it, "He just really felt like we are creating a new family and we should have the same name. It was about unity in the relationship for him. He wasn't thinking that I should take his name because I am his wife; it was really, just, let's all have the same name."

Franci's desire to keep her own name and her husband's desire for a family name led them both to take each other's name. As she expressed it, "The only problem is that people screw it up all the time. I don't think it is that hard to say two last names, but people invariably mix up which name comes first, or just say the last one. It hasn't quite worked out the way we envisioned it. Now we might go back to just each having our own names."

Another solution is for one partner to take the other's name. Mark and Rona both had well-established careers when they married. Both were clear that, professionally, they would keep their own names. They discussed many options. As Mark said, "We briefly discussed hyphenating our last names. But it just sounded awful! We discussed Rona taking my last name or my taking hers. In the end, I took her last name. Her family and its history meant so much to her, I was happy to take on the name as my own and pass it on to our children. I was really surprised how easy it was for me. My family name would be carried on through my brothers. When I told my friends and family, they responded with shock. But they've gotten used to it, and we're really pleased with our decision."

Jess and Sue followed a more common route. While each kept her own last name, they agreed that their children would have Jess's family name as a middle name and Sue's as a last name. As Sue said, "This way both names will have meaning for us and for our children."

While highly unusual, the following illustrates a unique solution to this problem. David Rosen and Jennie Castleman wanted to have the same family name to have a sense of family unity. But their hyphenated last names would be unwieldy. To their delight and surprise, after a little research, Jennie found their new family name. She had discovered that the grandmother for whom she had been named, quite remarkably, was Jennie Rosenn. David simply added another "n" to his name, and Jennie changed her name to Rosenn. Jennie did have to adopt an entirely new name, but she had a sense of reclaiming a part of her family's past. Jennie said, "It was a perfect solution. The only problem is you can't recommend it to your friends."

Discussing these issues now, when they are no longer theoretical, may produce some surprises for each of you.

Changing a Name

If you do choose to change your name, you may want to ask yourself how you are going to effect that transition. When couples change their name now, the change is most often conferred by the bandleader at the wedding reception: "And now, ladies and gentlemen, for the first time as husband and wife, Mr. and Mrs. Goldberg." Strangely, the bandleader, the Department of Motor Vehicles, and the Internal Revenue Service are often the three most proactive players in acknowledging a name change. Judaism would suggest, though, that to change your name requires more than an announcement—it requires a blessing.

Changing a name has been viewed both positively and negatively in Judaism. Tradition frowned upon changing a name in order to assimilate into non-Jewish culture. According to *Midrash T'hillim* 114:4, the Israelites deserved to be freed from Egyptian slavery because even though they lived in Egypt for 400 years, they had never adopted Egyptian names.

By and large, though, the Torah and other Jewish texts have a positive view of name changes. Symbolically, a changed name indicates a person's changed status. Abram's name was changed to Abraham when he was given the call to follow God. Sarai's name was changed to Sarah after she encountered God. Jacob's name was changed to Israel after he wrestled with the angel. An encounter with God transforms or confirms a new name. The Talmud (BT *Rosh HaShanah* 16b) teaches that a means of canceling a decree of death is to change your name. The name change insures a change of status from nearly dead to fully alive. In fact, based on this teaching, a custom arose among Ashkenazic Jews in the Middle Ages of changing the name of a gravely ill person in the hopes that the *Malach Hamavet,* the Angel of Death, would not be able to find the person, canceling the decree of death.

Jews have developed various methods for choosing a new name. Some people choose a name by flipping randomly through the Torah and selecting the first name they come across that is associated with a heroic or holy figure. Others give a sick person an auspicious name, like Chaim, meaning "life." Some think of a person whose life they want their own to resemble. Still others reflect on the meaning of a name and choose one that connotes characteristics they hope to embody.

A Traditional Blessing for Changing a Name

There is even a traditional blessing for changing a name:

> Our holy Rabbis said that four things cause an evil decree passed on a man to be canceled, one of them being the change of the sick person's name. We fulfilled what they said and his/her name was changed and it is a different person. Just as his/her name was changed, so may the evil decree pass on him/her, changing from decree to mercy, from death to life, from illness to a complete healing for [the person's new name].

Thank goodness you are not ill and you are not facing anything life-threatening. However, in a very real sense, you are hoping that you can positively affect your shared future in as many ways as possible. If either of you is going to change your name, consider effecting this change with a blessing.

A Contemporary Blessing for Changing a Name

The words of this blessing, while loosely based on tradition, are only one possibility. You can write or rewrite a blessing that expresses what your name change will mean to you.

> As Abraham and Sarah's names were changed when they encountered God, and as Jacob's name was changed when he wrestled with the angel, may my change of name from _____ [old name] to _____ [new name] symbolize the blessing of my changed status, the different person I am becoming in relation to my beloved, my family, friends, and God. Just as my name has changed, so may all harshness in my life change to mercy, may all death change to life, may all illness change to complete healing, and may all sadness change to joy.

If you will be changing your name when you marry, this blessing can be recited prior to, during, or after your wedding ceremony. Or, as is the custom for naming baby girls, you may want to consider using this blessing when you are next called to the Torah or when you are next at a Torah service or in a synagogue.

Exercise 27. Holding On and Letting Go

Part I

Separately, answer the following questions:
1. Would you consider changing your family name?
2. Why would you consider a name change?
3. What sense of loss might you feel with a name change?
4. What other emotions do you think a name change would evoke?
5. What would it mean to you to take on your partner's family name?
6. What do you see as possible new names for you as an individual?
7. What do you see as possible new names for your family?

Part II

Discuss your answers with your partner and see what decisions you can make.

✺ Conditions and Promises: Names ✺

Try to formulate a number of statements about the power that names have for you. Then articulate your conditions and promises related to names.

Finances: A Shared Bank Account
Can Be Scarier than a Shared Bedroom

> You can tell a person by three things: the way he holds his liquor,
> the way he gets angry, and the way he deals with money.
> BT *Eiruvin* 65b

The Rabbis of the Talmud understood that the way people deal with money reflects how they relate to other people and how other people perceive them. Issues related to money often bring out the demons in people. As you imagine your shared future, learning to understand how each of you relates to money and learning to communicate honestly about your financial concerns, fears, and needs will be of utmost importance.

Some couples spend their entire lives with different bank accounts, never merging their finances. Other couples combine finances from day one. Of course, other factors must also be considered as you determine how to deal with your money. These may include being a two-income family, coming into the relationship with debts or long-term financial obligations, anticipating major financial changes, having children, and buying a home. When you are figuring out how to deal with your money, the key for relationships is not the solution, but rather finding a process by which you can comfortably discuss, compromise, and work through issues that arise. Solutions will then follow.

Developing Attitudes toward Money

Consciously or unconsciously, you have adopted patterns that are a reaction to the environment in which you were raised. Exploring that world can provide both of you with greater insight into the habits, attitudes, and responses you have to each other's approaches to money, helping shape the way in which you will manage your money as you become a family. Some people relate to money in one way while single and in a radically different way when in a committed relationship. Certain habits, they believe, are the products or privileges of being young or unattached. They have no expectation that they will be lifelong habits. Others establish patterns at a very young age that they anticipate following throughout their lives. Ultimately, there is no single way to deal with money. What is important now for the two of you is to figure out what will be comfortable for you, being the specific individuals that you are.

Jean was raised in a home where her father imposed a strict allowance on her mother, who had chosen not to work while her children were young. Jean remembers how frustrated her mother was not having any control over the family's money. When Jean was a teenager, her parents divorced. Before the divorce proceedings, Jean's mother took all the money from the joint bank account she had with her husband and ran away with it, leaving her ex-husband in dire financial straits.

While dating, Jean always paid her own way. When she and Dave began to discuss living together, she was adamant about maintaining her own accounts. For Jean, who had seen the damage that money could cause, a shared bank account was far scarier than a shared bedroom. In anticipation of their wedding, Jean and Dave discussed how they would deal with their finances. Dave was clear. He wanted the two of them to pool their resources and have joint accounts and investments. Though Jean loved and trusted Dave more than anyone else in her life, she could simply not conceive of such an arrangement. For her, having access to money meant independence, autonomy, and freedom. She could imagine having some joint money, but there had to be some money that was just hers. Eventually, they agreed that when they married they would set up two types of accounts: each would have an individual account, and together they would have a joint account. Their paychecks would go into their individual accounts, from which they would contribute equal amounts to their joint account. From their individual accounts, they would pay personal bills, such as school and car loans and credit card bills. From their joint account, they would pay for household expenses, joint acquisitions, and vacations. They also agreed that each would keep assets that predated the marriage in their own names.

Jean wished she could just let go of her fears and follow Dave's lead. She, like he, had fantasies of a marriage in which everything was shared. Ultimately, what was important for Jean and Dave was recognizing and being able to communicate what they each needed and why they needed it. Understanding each other's histories and the emotions that money matters engendered enabled them to find a solution. Dave hoped this would be a temporary solution. Jean could make no such promise but was open to reevaluating their system after some time.

Isaac and Becca were like night and day when it came to thinking about money. Isaac had adopted the spending patterns of his mother, who was an extravagant spender and often lived beyond her means. He saw no reason for keeping records of his expenditures. The money he earned, he spent. And the occasional bounced check did not worry him. He carried some debt, "just like everyone else."

Becca, on the other hand, was thrifty. She came from a home where modest living and long-term saving were core values. She only let balances accrue on her credit cards to maintain a good credit rating, and she budgeted her expenses to pay off her student loans faster than necessary.

Becca and Isaac realized that, long-term, neither would be comfortable with the other's ways with money. So, they decided to try an experiment. Each of them would introduce the other to the joys of their approach. Maimonides, in his ethical tract *Sh'monah P'rakim* (Eight Chapters), wrote, "It is more difficult to teach someone who is a spendthrift to spend than it is to teach a carefree spender to save." So, Isaac prepared Becca for a shopping spree. He began by playing a game with her. She was to imagine things that if she had all the money in the world, she would consider buying. At first she was resistant, considering it a stupid and nearly impossible exercise. After a few weeks, with his constant coaxing, she started to imagine and share things she might like to have. One afternoon, he took her to a store. He literally walked her over to the things she had said she wanted, helped her take something off the shelf, stood in line with her at the cash register, and immediately took it out of its box for her to enjoy. When her guilt set in, Isaac reminded her that she was still going to be able to take care of all of her financial obligations for the month, even with this unanticipated, unnecessary expenditure.

Becca then sat down with Isaac and shared the pleasures she derived from imagining the life she and they would have in the future if they lived frugally now. She showed how planning made possible the complete abandon and escape she felt when they vacationed, because she knew it was not beyond her means. Neither was totally swayed by the other, but they did come to appreciate, in a new and deeper way, their very different perspectives and attitudes.

Jon rarely bought things, but he appreciated the comfortable life and surroundings that Beth's spending provided. Beth never kept receipts or recorded checks, while he liked to keep track of their expenses. Jon had no problem with Beth's spending money; all he wanted were records that reflected how much money was being spent. Rather than argue month after month over balancing their books, they found some mutually agreeable solutions to their widely differing approaches. They got a checkbook that made automatic carbon copies so that there would be records at the end of the month. And they always kept thousands of dollars easily accessible to cover unexpected large credit card bills. Fortunately, they were comfortable enough financially to make it work.

Exercise 28. Money

Discuss the following with each other:

1. Describe your parents' relationship with money as you were growing up. Were they spendthrifts? Risk takers?
2. Did your parents share a common approach to finances? If not, how did they manage things? What models did they provide for you about negotiating?
3. Share clichés that describe how your families viewed money.
4. Describe your own relationship with money. Do you know what influenced the way you relate to money?
5. Can you articulate how you and your partner's attitudes toward money differ?
6. How comfortable are you with each other's money management styles?

Determining Your Finances

Controlling the Money

> One who wishes to acquire wisdom should study the way money works, for there is no greater area of Torah study than this.
>
> BT *Bava Batra* 175b

Money is a highly emotional issue for so many people because of all that it represents. Acquiring and having access to money tap into issues of power, control, and security. As the two of you prepare to make joint financial decisions, you will need to determine what monies each of you will have access to and what control each of you will have over monies you earn and/or jointly use.

When Stacey and Mark married, they were both established professionals and had lived on their own for ten and fifteen years, respectively. Neither one had had to account for his or her financial habits to anyone. As Stacey said:

> I was thirty-five years old, and I had been working for ten years as a lawyer, making my own money, and being totally in charge of it. No one else spent any part of it but me. And then, after we moved in together and agreed to combine our finances, one day, my fiancé was going to the bank, and I had to literally hand over my paycheck to him. It was really difficult.

Stacey experienced the simple act of having someone else do banking for her as handing over her paycheck.

Stacey and Mark were of similar minds about finances. They were both diligent with their records and cognizant about income and expenditures. They also both wanted and needed to know exactly what was coming in and going out. Stacey remarked:

> Neither of us wanted to give up control—neither of us wanted to just say to the other, "OK, you take care of paying all the bills." Some people like being ignorant of the bills, like having someone do all the laundry, but we each needed to feel like we were in control. On the other hand, neither of us wanted total control over our finances. That would be too much pressure.

They understood and respected each other's needs and fears. As a result, they created a solution, which quickly became a family ritual. They sit down on a biweekly basis to discuss financial matters, pay bills, and review calendars. For Stacey and Mark, committing themselves to spending time together in this way helped allay both of their concerns about the control of money. Like Stacey and Mark, you will benefit from finding your own way to discuss the issue of money rather than be silent or ignore it.

Changing Times, Changing Roles

The following are the kinds of work a wife must perform for her husband: grinding wheat, baking bread, washing clothes, cooking, nursing her child, making her husband's bed, and working in wool.

BT K'tubot 59b

Remarkably, the Talmud's prescribed gender roles endured for countless centuries. With the entry of women into the workplace and an increasing number of same-gender couples, gender roles have been dramatically redefined. The issues of who will be the primary wage earner, who will take care of the kids, and who will make any necessary career sacrifices are open questions for many couples. Not having clear roles and expectations can be disconcerting, especially for those men who have grown up with more traditional views of work, family, and money. An honest discussion of the roles you each plan on fulfilling can be an important building block in your developing relationship.

Betty and Lance met when they were both Ph.D. candidates. They were each dedicated to their fields and dreamed of teaching at a university level. They knew jobs were scarce. But, they wanted to—needed to—believe that everything would work out. They decided they would take turns moving, each allowing the other's career to take precedence at times. When they completed their Ph.D.'s, like so many other two-profession families, they found it almost impossible to find two desirable full-time jobs in the same city.

> In some ways our [first] solution was very simplistic. We just
> decided to take turns. I went first, leading her to a school in Tulsa,
> where she had a part-time job. After a few years, it became clear
> that it was time for me to move on.

By this point, Betty and Lance had a few kids. And, as they had long
ago agreed, it was Betty's turn to put her career first. Suddenly, Lance
found himself being the kids' primary caretaker and looking for a
part-time job. He and Betty were stunned to find that Lance's whole
sense of self was challenged when he had to act out his egalitarian beliefs.

> I would say, coming from a generation of men who while experi-
> encing themselves to be certainly more liberated than their par-
> ents and believing in egalitarianism, I still had preconceived
> notions of what men do. Consequently, when I was leaving that
> first job, Betty looked at me and said, "Now it's my time." We had
> one discussion, where I said, "Are you sure?" And she gave me a
> look, which said, "Are you crazy? We had a deal." I quickly said,
> "I was just kidding." But in reality my heart sank a little, because
> some of my psyche still wanted to be the primary breadwinner.
> Soon after, she got a great job. And I found myself having moved
> to a new city, where I did not have a job, and it was at times a
> humbling and at times a really depressing experience.

Lance's identity was tied up with his being out in the community,
functioning as primary breadwinner, and being employed. He didn't
know what to do with his sense of frustration and jealousy as he
watched Betty and her career blossom. He realized that while he was
fully wrapped up in his career, he had lost sight of how Betty felt, working just part-time, deferring her career dreams. While it had its pitfalls,
they came to the conclusion that, for them, the simple idea of following each other was pretty much the only way they could have done it.

As you build your relationship, figuring out your work and family
priorities and your role expectations is essential. As Lance said:

> To not talk about it is to get nailed by a time bomb. You have to
> have some sort of agreement or protocol for how the roles are
> going to work out so you both feel comfortable.

Long-Range Planning

Although it may seem too early in your relationship to discuss issues like retirement, the fact is that planning for retirement, making a will, and getting life insurance can all be important pieces of your financial life, pieces you should begin to address now.

Judy had always put money aside for her retirement. She worked with a financial advisor who helped her make long-term investments. She looked forward to having a home of her own and raising children. She had every expectation that they would go to college and that she would cover the cost. Jennifer also expected to have money for retirement for herself and her mate. But she was young—she'd think about that in a few years. For now, she wanted to enjoy her job, which paid well, take advantage of her youth, and slowly, as slowly as legally possible, pay back her student loans. She believed that if all continued on its current trajectory, they could easily make their short- and long-term dreams a reality. Judy loved Jennifer's carefree attitude, but as the reality of a shared future became clearer, she wanted the two of them to figure out what their financial future might look like.

Jeff and Amy sat down to discuss their future. Jeff spoke of the traveling they would do, the savings he anticipated, and the cost of college educations. Amy jumped in and said, "We can't forget about Eric. You know I've promised my parents that I will take care of him when they die!" Jeff knew this intellectually, as Amy had long ago told him about it. But, now, it had to become part of his plans, their plans. Amy's parents had earned and saved enough to maintain themselves and Eric, their developmentally disabled son. However, their savings were modest. Eric's physical health was good, and everyone knew he would never be self-supporting. Amy had always assumed that she would forgo certain dreams and luxuries to ensure her brother's safety and comfort. Now she and Jeff had to figure out how they would work things out.

Josh and Marilyn had both been married before. They spoke often and at length about their kids and the ways they hoped to merge the lives of their two families. Marilyn and her ex-husband had long ago agreed that he would cover the kids' college tuition. Josh, however, now felt that he wanted to pay for their college educations to make a clear statement that he considered them his own children. Josh's parents were well-to-do. Neither Josh nor his siblings needed to anticipate having future financial obligations for their parents' care. Marilyn's parents, on the other hand, were living on a fixed income. She and her sister had always expected to equally share the expenses of maintaining their parents in a comfortable lifestyle in their old age. Josh and Marilyn realized they still had a lot to discuss and work through.

The Ketubah—*A Jewish Prenuptial Agreement*

As more and more couples are marrying late in life, they are coming into a marriage with both assets and debts. Alan and Liz had each entered their marriage with financial assets. Alan's assets were in stocks that he held with his family. Prior to their wedding, they signed a prenuptial agreement, stating that the assets they each held at the start of their marriage would remain exclusively theirs in the case of death or divorce. However, anything they earned during the marriage they would share.

The use of a prenuptial agreement is obviously a difficult decision. In the words of a lawyer who handles them, "Many prenuptial agreements are done in the week before the wedding and can have a chilling effect upon the marriage if seen as a sign of distrust."

Alan, however, had a different perspective on his prenuptial agreement.

> The motivation for signing the agreement was to safeguard the assets for the family, having nothing to do with the assets that we make together. As much as I was in love with my wife, when we got engaged, I had to take seriously the reality that we live in a society where people say to each other, all the time, "I love you and I want to spend the rest of my life with you," and then get divorced a year later. We needed to be realistic.
>
> Having said that, there was a trace of bad faith that the document brought up for both of us. It seemed to stain the *k'dushah* [holiness] of the *chuppah* [wedding], by planning for a divorce. But it hasn't gotten in the way of anything. We are coming up on being together four years. We're incredibly joyous that we have never thought about it. But the very idea of planning for divorce or death comes from Jewish tradition and the *ketubah* itself.

Alan's last comment may surprise you. But it's true. The traditional Jewish marriage contract, the *ketubah*, is primarily a financial document, an ancient form of a prenuptial agreement. Though it mentions cherishing and honoring, it primarily speaks of money and property. The *ketubah*, as it was initially formulated, was a profoundly important, even revolutionary, document in terms of women's rights. The traditional *ketubah* provides that, in the case of divorce or death, the woman will receive a financial settlement. In the ancient world, women were completely dependent upon men for sustenance; they couldn't hold jobs, their inheritance rights were limited, and they had little economic power. Thus, the *ketubah*'s declaration that, upon divorce or death, the woman would receive money gave her certain power in the relationship and guaranteed her economic security.

Although originally a document meant to protect women, the traditional *ketubah* is highly problematic for many modern, liberal Jews today. Through it, the man is effectively purchasing the woman, with her purchase price dependent on her status as a virgin. It stipulates the amount of money the man agrees to pay in case of divorce or death. Two male witnesses testify that the man, not the woman or the couple, has agreed to the terms. The woman is discussed, but she has no voice in the discussion. Liberal Jews have taken the original concept of the *ketubah* and created alternative contemporary egalitarian *k'tubot* that focus primarily on a couple's mutual love and commitment, hopes and plans, rather than on finances.

However, while the non-egalitarian nature of the traditional *ketubah* may cause you to dismiss it entirely, it may be valuable to consider the merits of such an unromantic prenuptial agreement. While you will hopefully never need to turn to it, given the prevalence of divorce in today's world, discussing your perceptions about the property and assets you currently hold as well as about your future earnings can be a big help.

Is it healthy pragmatism to negotiate financial matters before the wedding, or does it inject doubt into the relationship? Judaism historically took pragmatism over romance. Fortunately, today you don't need to choose between the two. Whether or not you choose to have a prenuptial agreement, a healthy pragmatism about money means recognizing what your partner expects financially out of the marriage, which requires both of you to get beyond any fears you may have about talking about finances.

If you are a same-sex couple, you will have to make special arrangements to insure that your financial and legal bonds are secure. Once married, a heterosexual couple enjoys a host of benefits, from inheritance to decision-making rights in the case of sudden incapacity. Same-sex couples do not enjoy these same rights unless they draw up specific legal documents. To give legal weight to your commitment to each other, contact the Lambda Legal Defense and Education Fund, a national organization with chapters around the country. Their legal staff is familiar with local, state, and federal laws that can protect you as a couple.

Exercise 29. Budgeting

Part I

Prepare, in writing, a guess/estimate of what your partner spends monthly on the following:

1. Clothing
2. Food at lunch
3. CDs/Videos/DVDs
4. Books/computer equipment
5. Household items
6. Car payments
7. School loan payments

Part II

Compare your lists. Share your actual expenditures. Share your reactions and your comfort levels with the information you've received.

Exercise 30. Expectations

Discuss the following questions with each other:

1. Who is the primary breadwinner currently, and do you expect that to remain the case?

2. How comfortable is each of you with your current roles? Does the current situation mirror your childhood expectations? Elaborate.
3. How much do you have to earn to be content and comfortable?
    a) Are your answers similar?
    b) Do either or both of you have expectations that this will change over time?
        1) If so, how?
        2) If not, how will you deal with shifts that occur?

Exercise 31. Borrowing and Lending

Discuss the following questions with each other:

1. How do you feel about borrowing and lending?
2. If you have borrowed money:
    a) How did you feel?
    b) Why did you choose or need to borrow?
    c) Did it work out as you expected?
3. When have you loaned money?
    a) How did you feel?
    b) Did it work out as you expected?
4. To whom would you feel comfortable turning if you needed a loan?
5. To whom would you feel obligated or have a strong desire to lend money if asked?

Exercise 32. Picturing Your Financial Future

Part I

Separately, make a list of your financial goals and obligations, including acquisitions, college funds, savings, investments, retirement options, etc.

Part II

Make separate lists of your anticipated future financial obligations.

Part III

Review your own list and, particularly with regard to acquisitions, consider the time frame in which you would like to be able to achieve your financial goals.

Part IV

Share your lists with each other and take note of what things are similar or different, including time frames.

Exercise 33. Financial Fears

Part I

Separately, write down the following:

1. Financial possibilities that most frighten you and concern you.
2. Ways to avert the possibility of your fears becoming reality.

Part II

Share what you wrote. Don't argue. Listen carefully.

Exercise 34. Financial Fantasies: "If I could set up our finances, we'd . . ."

Part I

Write down how you would set up your mutual finances, if you could.

Part II

Share what you wrote with each other. Repeat back to each other what you have heard, what parts of the plan resonate with you, and which parts are problematic.

Part III

Discuss with each other what you would do if you won the lottery and suddenly had an extra $30,000.

1. What do your answers tell you about each other?
2. Could you have predicted each other's answers?

Exercise 35. Insurance, Wills, and Prenuptial Agreements

Discuss the following questions with each other:

1. When you get married, you may have new options for insurance (e.g., health, life).
    a) What insurance does each of you currently have?
    b) Why did you get it?
    c) How will you make your decisions about your insurance options?
    d) How important does each of you feel health, life, and long-term health care insurance to be?
2. Do either of you have a will?
    a) What are its contents?
    b) How did you choose your executor and your beneficiaries?
    c) How will your will change after you marry? Whose decision do you believe it should be?
    d) What sorts of financial stipulations would you want to include in a will?
3. Do you want a formal prenuptial agreement?
    a) Why? Why not?
    b) Should you seek advice about this?

Exercise 36. How Shall We Do Our Financial Planning?

Review your responses to exercises 29 through 35. If you find that you generally agree with each other, do you have clear ideas of how to work toward achieving your common goals? If the exercises underscored sources of current or potential conflicts, how can you constructively address and resolve them? Do either or both of you have a background in finance or financial planning?

Many couples find it very helpful to consult a professional before they make decisions about consolidating assets and debts, about bank accounts and investments, and about insurance, wills, and prenuptials agreements.

Money as a Means to Create Holiness within Your Relationship

Bills, debts, control of finances—there are so many issues surrounding money that can be a source of stress and difficulty in a relationship. Jewish tradition also reminds us that money can be a source of holiness, through the giving of *tzedakah*. *Tzedakah* is often defined simply as "charity." Yet charity implies something done out of the goodness of the giver's heart; while, for the Jew, *tzedakah* is an obligation. The *Shulchan Aruch* (in *Yoreh Dei-ah* 251:12) states that even a poor person who is kept alive by *tzedakah* funds must give *tzedakah* from what he receives.

Rabbi Nachman of Bratzlav said:

> *Tzedakah* has the power to widen the entrance to holiness. When a person wants to embark upon a certain path of devotion, he [or she] first needs to make an opening in order to enter into this new path. This is why all beginnings are difficult. But giving *tzedakah* makes the entrance wider.
>
> *Likutei Moharan* 2:4,1–2

Giving *tzedakah* is therefore not considered an onerous obligation; rather it is seen as a vehicle for edification, for reaching a higher spiritual level.

To live as a Jew is to live beyond the personal sphere. It is to live as a member of the human community, reaching beyond oneself and one's family to help others. According to the midrash, when Jacob met Rachel at the well, the waters of the well surged up and overflowed onto all the fields of the land. Their meeting resulted in the whole town benefiting from the newly watered fields (*Pirkei D'Rabbi Eliezer* 36). Your relationship can also overflow and come to benefit other people. Regularly giving *tzedakah* is one way for your relationship to overflow and water the fields around you.

The following are suggestions for making money a path to holiness in your relationship:

1. Jewish homes traditionally have a *tzedakah* box in a visible place in the home. You may want to make it a custom in your new family to give some amount of money to *tzedakah* every week. You can create a special tradition for this in your family (e.g., at dinner once a week, perhaps before Shabbat).
2. Your engagement party and wedding provide opportunities for *tzedakah*. You can:
   a. Ask people, on the invitations, to make charitable donations in lieu of gifts.
   b. Place a *tzedakah* box on each table or at the door, to encourage people to think of others as they celebrate your joy with you.
   c. Make arrangements with a local food pantry to pick up leftover food after your party.
   d. Donate 3 percent of what you spend on catering to Mazon, an organization that funds hunger programs throughout the country, or another organization that provides food for the hungry.
   e. Choose an alternative to flower arrangements on tables, such as books and toiletries that can be brought to a homeless shelter.

Giving *tzedakah* during your engagement period can help you establish it as a regular practice in the home you share. It is especially appropriate during your engagement; Jews traditionally give *tzedakah* to acknowledge joyous occasions, by bringing a little more joy into someone else's life. Also, engagement is traditionally understood as a time of reflection and atonement. Giving *tzedakah* is traditionally used for these purposes as well.

Who Is Rich?

Though the bulk of this chapter has focused on money matters, a more fundamental question about wealth remains. The Mishnah, in *Pirkei Avot* 4:1, asks, "Who is rich?" The first response is "The one who rejoices in his lot." In the Talmud, Rabbi Akiva answers the same question by saying, "He who has a wife who is becoming in all of her actions" (BT *Shabbat* 25b). While Rabbi Akiva's comment obviously reflects a patriarchal view, the essence of his comment is worth noting. Your own wealth can be measured by the actions of your partner. Conversely, you must also remember that your actions reflect on your partner; in this relationship, there is mutual responsibility. Ultimately, as *Sefer Maalot HaMidot* explains, Judaism's relationship with money is as follows:

> Despise not riches. Honor the wealthy if they are benevolent and modest. But remember that the true riches is contentment.
> Morris Joseph, *Judaism as Creed and Life* (1910)

There are many opportunities for money to drive a wedge between a couple and create a stressful environment in a marriage. It is important for you to help each other remember the nonmaterial things that make you and your lives rich.

Exercise 37. How Are You Rich? How Is Your Life Rich?

Part I

Separately, prepare the following lists:

1. Things that enrich your life.
2. Ways that your partner enriches your life.

Part II

Share your lists with each other.

Part III

Discuss the following questions with each other:

1. Five years from now, what do you anticipate will add to the richness of your life?
2. How can you help each other make it possible?

⚛ Conditions and Promises: Financial Expectations ⚛

Try to formulate a number of statements that express your notions about "Who is rich?"

Try to formulate some statements that capture the expectations and needs you each have about money, the conditions you feel comfortable establishing at this point in time regarding your finances, and the promises you will try to uphold with and for each other related to finances.

7

Religion: Asking Life's Big Jewish Questions

We're Both Jewish—What's the Problem?

Josh and Cheryl were engaged to be married and had been going through a process of engagement counseling with their rabbi. When it came time to plan the actual details of the wedding, they got stuck on whether they wanted the traditional *ketubah* or a liberal, contemporary version. The rabbi explained that the traditional *ketubah* was, to a large extent, a financial document; while the liberal version, using dramatically altered language and concepts, speaks of the couple's shared love, commitment, and hopes. After detailing the function and meaning of the *ketubah* at Jewish weddings, the rabbi asked them which one they would prefer. Cheryl immediately said, "The alternative version!" only to hear Josh say, at that exact same moment, "The traditional one!"

Neither Josh nor Cheryl was particularly observant. Yet, they quickly realized that the seemingly simple question about *ketubah* style touched deep chords in each of them. Their discussion about this symbol forced them to articulate their relationship to Judaism and Jewish traditions in greater depth than ever before. Josh wanted a ceremony that was "authentically Jewish," meaning one that included long-standing traditions and symbols. Cheryl wanted a ceremony in which every symbol had meaning for her and for them as a couple. Josh was proud to be Jewish and felt traditional prayers and symbols would reinforce his sense of connection to Jewish memory and history. Cheryl's Judaism was rooted in the present. She only engaged in rituals that had meaning for her in her daily life. She, therefore, liked the idea of having a *ketubah* but rejected the idea of using a formula that reflected an understanding of women and marriage that bore no resemblance to her own modern understandings and life patterns.

When asked to look deeper and determine why they both felt the way they did, they found they were each searching for answers. Like so many couples, they had both assumed that as two Jews there was no need for a formal discussion about religion. However, when they heard each other's reponses, they realized the *ketubah* was only one of the many issues they should plan to discuss. This conversation marked the beginning of their thinking about and sharing their spiritual and Jewish lives with each other.

Tachlis: Moving from Ideas to Practice

> Many couples make the mistake of waiting to talk about religious issues until after their engagement—I think this is setting yourselves up for failure. Getting swept away with falling in love without dealing with the *tachlis* of how you want to run your home and what part you want religion to play is ignoring an important reality in life.
>
> Chaya, 29, recently married

In Yiddish, *tachlis* means substance. Colloquially, "talking *tachlis*" means getting down to the nitty-gritty. It is important for you to explore the *tachlis* religious issues in your own lives in the here and now. You are talking about a lifetime together. How you choose to express your identity as Jews, your participation in rituals and observances, and your communal involvements will have a significant impact on your short- and long-term relationship.

When Greg and Laura got engaged, they knew they loved each other, but they were both concerned about the frequent conflicts they had about religious observance. Ironically, they anticipated the arrival of Shabbat, a day for rest and relaxation, with great stress and trepidation. They both came from families that did not routinely observe Shabbat and had continued their families' practices through their college and graduate school years. After business school, though, Greg became friendly with a group of more traditionally observant Jews. When he joined them in their observance of Shabbat—going to synagogue, having Shabbat dinner, lighting candles, making *Havdalah*—he found a part of his soul was profoundly touched. Soon, whether or not he was with friends, he went to synagogue and performed the Shabbat home rituals for himself.

When Laura met Greg, he had been observing Shabbat in this manner for a number of years. Laura was not against observing Shabbat, but when she did, she was never personally moved by the experience. Before they were engaged, and even after, Laura experienced Greg's Shabbat observances as an imposition. She often wanted to go out to dinner or do something with friends on a Friday night, while Greg wanted to go to *shul*. When they traveled, their time away was often filled with anger and frustration. Prior to leaving, Laura investigated things to see and do; Greg always wanted to be near a synagogue so he could go to services. He also wanted restaurants where he could order fish or vegetarian food. Laura often found herself touring alone, and Greg often found himself well beyond walking distance from a synagogue.

Slowly, through the course of many conversations, they found a balance they could both live with. Laura came to appreciate their home celebrations of Shabbat and holidays. Greg became less stringent about his expectations when they traveled. Greg said, "I was very conscious of not pushing her in any kind of observance way. I wanted her to share my ideas of Shabbat, but I tried not to force it. It had to be on her own terms."

When Ellen told Steven about how much youth group had meant to her, Steven listened attentively. But he couldn't relate at all. His high school years had been spent in such a different way. He knew he was Jewish. He'd become a bar mitzvah, though his parents had never really told him why it was so important to them. It certainly hadn't been meaningful to him. Prior to meeting Ellen, his bar mitzvah had been the last time he had been in a synagogue. Now, he was learning that the woman he loved not only had had a very different relationship with Judaism, she had actually chosen to make it the center of her social world as a teenager. She looked forward to their settling in a community, joining a synagogue, and reconnecting with Jewish life in a more meaningful way. Not only that, she couldn't wait to introduce their children to Judaism, to Jewish holidays and practices. She even fantasized that they would find youth group as meaningful as she had. It was one thing, Steven thought, for Ellen to look back nostalgically. It was another thing altogether for her to anticipate such an intense reconnection in the future. He realized, and hoped she did too, that they still had a lot to talk about.

Your differences may not be as extreme as Greg and Laura's or Ellen and Steven's, but now is the time to discuss both your responses to each other's practices and your expectations for the future.

Exercise 38. Your Jewish Upbringing

Separately, answer the following questions. Then share your answers with each other.

1. How would you characterize your parents' identities as Jews?
2. How did they choose to express it (e.g., joining a synagogue, giving to charity, supporting Israel, working to preserve the memory of the Holocaust or the communities destroyed in it, reading Jewish books, going to Jewish cultural events, intentionally distancing themselves from the organized Jewish world)?
3. How would you characterize your parents' religious practices?
4. Were your parents' religious beliefs and practices similar? If not:
   a. How did they negotiate any differences that they had?
   b. What tensions did they engender in your family?
   c. What confusion or ambivalence did their differences engender in you?
5. How and where were holidays celebrated?
   a. Was synagogue attendance part of holiday celebrations?
   b. Were your parents the hosts for family dinners, or did you go elsewhere?
   c. How would you describe the religious content of family holiday gatherings?
6. Did your family ever celebrate Shabbat?
   a. With what regularity? What was done?
   b. What influenced your families' (dis)engagement with Shabbat rituals?

Exercise 39. Your Jewish Identity

Discuss with your partner your answers to the following questions:

1. What does being Jewish mean to you?
2. How important is Jewish tradition in your life?
3. What parts of Jewish tradition are meaningful for you and why?
4. Would you define your Jewish identity in cultural, historical, ethnic, and/or religious terms?
5. How important is Jewish identity in your life?
6. How do you see your Judaism reflected in your daily life? In your life choices? In your understanding of the world? In your values?

Exercise 40. Your Partner's Family's Practices

Separately, answer the following questions for yourself. Then share your answers with your partner.

1. How comfortable are you with the Jewish ritual practices of your future in-laws?
   a. Are their rituals familiar to you?
   b. Are you comfortable celebrating Jewish holidays with them?
2. Are they respectful of your religious practices?
3. How have you dealt with the different practices of your families of origin?
4. How do you decide with whom you will spend holidays?

Exercise 41. Your Personal Practice

Part I

Discuss with your partner the following questions:

1. What Jewish rituals do you currently observe? Make a list and next to them mark "always," "frequently," "sometimes," or "rarely."
2. Why do you do these specific things?
3. How long have you done them?
4. What meaning do they have for you?

Part II

Separately, take time to answer the following questions. Then share your answers with each other.

1. What Jewish rituals would you like to observe in the home you establish together?
2. Why do you want to observe these specific rituals?
3. What will observing these rituals look like?
4. How comfortable are you with your partner's ways of connecting to things Jewish and your partner's level of ritual observance?
5. In an ideal world, what would you like to be the resolution of your differences?
6. How would you feel giving up some of these practices?
7. How important is it for you to share Jewish practices and observances?
8. How comfortable would you be, in the long run, to have very different practices?
9. If you plan to have children, how important is it to you for there to be a uniform set of practices that you model?

Conditions and Promises: Religious Observance

Try to articulate a few statements that capture your conditions and expectations regarding religious practices and observances. Then compose a few statements that express the promises you are ready to make in this area.

We're Not Both Jewish—Is It a Problem?

Interfaith Engagement

Melissa and Will walked slowly into the rabbi's office. She was in her fortieth week of pregnancy, and her baby was due any minute. Nervously, Will said, "Rabbi, we came to talk to you about the baby. We know it's going to be a boy, and we, *well really I*, would like to have him circumcised." Melissa was scared by the prospect of her eight-day-old baby boy having his foreskin removed in a public ritual. She said, "It's just that we never really talked about having a circumcision, and now Will suddenly feels like his child has to have one." The rabbi asked them to share with him their expectations for their child's religious upbringing. Will said hesitantly:

> Well, we haven't really done that much planning for it. Melissa agreed to raise our children Jewish, but I guess we really didn't go into what that meant. I wasn't even sure what it meant. Now that our son is on the way, I have no doubts it means he'll be circumcised.

Melissa shook her head, dismayed, and said, "I just don't know, I just don't know."

It may seem strange that a couple would wait until moments before childbirth to decide whether they would celebrate a *b'rit milah* (circumcision), but in fact it happens quite often. In the early stages of a relationship, couples often choose to ignore the importance of their religious attachments, even playing down their differences in an effort to celebrate their similarities. By doing so, they put off the inevitable. By burying their differences, they fail to understand that these differences do not cease to exist. Instead, they will surface at another time, often causing great conflict and hurt.

Confronting your religious differences and those of your extended families is an essential building block in your relationship. Before you decided to make a lifelong commitment to each other, you could join each other at religious celebrations as a guest. Now that you will be one family, expectations—yours and those of other family members—are likely to change. Ignoring these issues will only mean that they are deferred; they are not going to go away. Rather than being blindsided by them or dealing with recurring conflicts each time a holiday or ritual marking a life passage occurs, you can do yourselves a big favor by starting these discussions now.

"In Everyone's Eyes, I Was 'As Jewish As Jewish Can Be'"

Dana grew up in a very strongly identified Jewish family. Her mom was president of the synagogue sisterhood, and even though they rarely went to services, Judaism was central to the family's identity. Dana always felt intensely connected to the synagogue and its rituals. She pleaded with her parents to have a bat mitzvah and was the only girl in her family to have one. "When I was in my teens, Judaism was a coat that I threw around myself to comfort me, it was so important to me. I was the one in the family who dragged everybody else to *shul*." Given this, everyone was surprised when Dana found herself in college deeply involved with Bob McNamee.

> After we were married, when I went back to my high school for a reunion and my last name was McNamee, people were shocked. In everyone's eyes, I was "as Jewish as Jewish can be." I did try really hard to find a nice Jewish boy. When I was dating Bob, I broke up with him at one point and tried to make a last effort to find someone Jewish, but I just kept coming back to him; he was the one.

When Dana and Bob got engaged, one of the main issues they dealt with as an interfaith couple was their parents. Bob's parents, devout Catholics, were very upset. His mother worried that the souls of her Jewish grandchildren would not be saved. Bob's mother told him, flat out, that he shouldn't marry Dana. Dana and Bob dismissed her concerns but were troubled by her convictions and worried about what their marriage would do to their relationship with Bob's parents. Dana's parents got over their initial shock, welcomed Bob, and hoped that he would come to feel comfortable at their Jewish celebrations. They convinced themselves that Dana's children would, of course, be raised as Jews. But they never discussed their expectations with Dana and Bob.

Tales are told of parents disowning their children because of an interfaith marriage. However, such an extreme response is no longer the norm. Parental unhappiness may be due as much to family structure and dynamics as it is to loyalty to a particular religious or ethnic tradition. Your family's ability to accept the choices you make for yourself is often a direct reflection of how well they have accepted your status as an independent, autonomous adult. Rabbi Neil Kominsky, who works extensively with interfaith couples, says:

> If you have two families of absolutely equal commitment to Jewish life, one family, when finding out their child is going to marry someone who is not Jewish, will threaten sitting shivah, and never seeing their child again, while the other family will say this is not what we planned but we will make the best of it. Why the difference? What is probably going on has more to do with families' granting autonomy to their children to make adult choices than it does with religion. (Interview by author)

While religion can be a factor, quite often the ultimate issues are trust and autonomy. This works both ways, however. Often, parents are not the only ones working through these issues. To enter a marriage, you have to be comfortable with your identity as an independent adult ready to commit to and trust in your new family, independent of the wishes and desires of your parents. Rabbi Kominsky describes this phenomenon in the following way:

> If a couple finds themselves questioning their decision to get married because of a parent's religious objections, the couple might want to rethink getting married. One of the definitions of marriage in our society is that you don't need a parent's permission. If your parents are able to cloud your mind, then you might not have been clear about getting married anyway, and you should think again. If a couple is clear about getting married and their parents are simply causing upheaval, if it is the Jewish parents, I recommend that they talk to me or to their own rabbi. (Interview by author)

Talking to a spiritual leader may be an important part of assuaging the concerns of a parent. Almost all rabbis in the Reform, Reconstructionist, and Conservative branches of Judaism will counsel parents that it is better to try and work out their relationship with their child than to make dramatic threats of cutting them off if they marry someone non-Jewish.

But What Will the Kids Be?

When Bob and Dana were engaged, the biggest question on their minds, as it is for most interfaith couples, was "How will we raise our kids?" Dana recalled the conversation: "I asked Bob if he would raise the kids as Jews, and he said, 'I don't have the child in my arms, but right now, I feel like it would be fine to raise our children as Jews.'" It wasn't a problem for Bob to agree to raise Jewish kids, but he did put a caveat in his response that is so important for interfaith families. He said that he felt *at the time* that it would not be a problem to raise Jewish children, but having a baby in his arms might make a difference. As an interfaith couple, you need to be open to the possibility that your feelings about certain issues may change over time. Bob and Dana had a verbal contract of sorts that they would raise their kids as Jews. And, as all couples do, they spent years, as new circumstances arose, renegotiating their contract.

Part of Bob and Dana's initial agreement was that there was going to be no celebration of Christmas in their home. Dana was adamant that bringing up Jewish children left no possibility of bringing any piece of Christian culture into their house. Bob was agreeable to it, because they would go and celebrate Christmas at his parents' home. But Bob's father passed away after their second child was born. Bob told Dana he felt orphaned and that he missed his father, and he was hoping that they could celebrate Christmas in the house for him. Dana responded by saying that there was no way she could have anything related to Christmas in her home. For Dana, having a Christmas tree meant that she had somehow failed: "The image of my kids not being Jewish, to this day, makes me think of dead relatives rolling over in their graves." She feared that giving any ground on this issue would compromise her children's Jewishness; not having strongly identified Jewish children would be a sign to herself, her parents, and her grandparents that she had failed as a parent and as a Jew.

Bob was struggling with a different set of issues. As he put it, "When I said I would bring the kids up Jewish, I did not really know what it meant. But when I realized what it meant, I began to feel left out." Bob had no problem with his children being Jewish. He did, however, have serious problems with his discomfort in being a member of a family that wasn't unified and one in which he didn't feel support for his religious choices. The celebration of Christmas in his home forced him to clarify for himself what his role in his family was.

Bob and Dana realized that, for them, it was time to renegotiate their contract. Together, they needed to redefine what it meant to raise Jewish kids and what place some sort of Christmas celebration might have in their home. They agreed to have a Christmas tree in their home, understanding they would be very clear with the children that the family was helping Bob celebrate Christmas. Bob also gave the children presents at Christmas, identifying it as his family's custom, not a religious celebration. They felt able to make this change because together they were giving their children the same simple message— mom and the kids are Jews, dad is Christian.

They were also able to reach a compromise about the Christmas tree because of Bob's clear, active role in raising the children as Jews. The kids had begun to attend Hebrew school, and Bob and Dana took turns schlepping them back and forth. As Bob grew more comfortable in and around the synagogue, he started going to events, helped out on committees, and began to study Judaism. If his children and wife were Jews, he wanted to understand the religion and culture that was theirs. Bob understood this was not the kind of religious unity he had always thought he would have. But this was a sacrifice he promised to make when he married Dana. Dana recognized that having a Christmas tree was not a reflection on her abilities or identity as a mother or a Jew. Her love and respect for Bob helped her make the compromises that would make their lives more meaningful. Their ability to successfully renegotiate rested on their ability to communicate with each other and compromise, when necessary.

A Thousand Issues and Four Keys for Working Them Out

John and Barbara spent hours and hours discussing the children they hoped to have. Barbara wanted to raise her children as Jews, but John had misgivings. John said, "I go to mass ten times more often than

Barbara ever goes to synagogue, so I was not really sure why it was so important to her. She said it was about perpetuating the tradition. And so I said, if perpetuating the tradition is so important, why don't you take a more active role in a synagogue or in Jewish observance?" For non-Jewish partners, it can be difficult to understand a partner's attachment to Judaism. Jewish identity—cultural, historical, or ethnic—is often foreign and perplexing for a non-Jewish partner.

John ultimately agreed to Barbara's request that they raise any children they have as Jews, even though he felt this might be difficult for him because he feared feeling isolated from their religious lives.

There were four keys for John and Barbara in working through this issue. First, Barbara was always clear and up front about her need to raise the kids Jewish. As John said, "It would be very difficult if we had become very involved emotionally with one another and then it came up. This was something that was discussed all along, to differing degrees, but it wasn't a bombshell at the end. It wasn't that we decided to get married and then she said, well there is just this one other thing." It does no good to hide your true feelings. By being open and honest you give yourselves more time to work through an issue, and you can avoid the unpleasant and emotionally charged decisions experienced by so many couples.

To communicate well with each other, you must first understand your own feelings and commitments. Barbara knew she wanted to raise her children as Jews, but many people who think they do not have strong feelings about religion and child rearing when discussing it in the abstract find that when they have a child they desperately want it to be welcomed into the world with specific religious rituals, such as circumcision or baptism. Try to be as truthful with yourself as possible in determining whether you need to raise your children in your religion, and be clear with your partner about your feelings.

The second key was confidence. Barbara was worried that John was not going to actively participate in raising the children as Jews, and John was worried that Barbara did not fully understand the sacrifice he was making by having his kids raised in a faith that was not his own. Barbara needed to feel confident that John was not going to say, "That's fine. You can raise the children as Jews, but I will not have anything to do with it, because I'm not Jewish."

If you do decide to raise your children as Jews, how will you both support that decision? Many non-Jewish partners in interfaith marriages ask, "How can a non-Jewish parent raise a Jewish child?" Reform Judaism believes it can be done. Through reading, studying, and gaining familiarity and comfort with Jewish rituals and customs, a non-Jewish parent can reinforce what a child learns. Moreover, the attitude that the parent conveys as a child participates in specifically Jewish activities will either support or undermine the seeds of identity that are growing. Before you have children, you can begin to discuss your commitments and expectations about raising your children in a specific religion.

It's in the home and in the daily lives of their children where non-Jewish parents may feel left out. But non-Jewish parents can participate in a myriad of ways: learning to lead some of the Shabbat blessings, helping build a sukkah, or reading along with children as they do homework for religious school. Part of this process will entail learning more about Judaism. The Union of American Hebrew Congregations holds classes throughout North America called "Introduction to Judaism." These courses are designed to introduce adults, Jews and non-Jews, to basic Jewish concepts. Similar courses are also offered through synagogues and Jewish community centers. If the non-Jewish parent makes a commitment to try to be a part of his/her child's religious life, it can be done. As rabbis, we know that some of the most committed parents in synagogues are non-Jewish parents who want their children to have a solid religious upbringing.

For a couple who is engaged and making the commitment to raise Jewish kids, the most important thing to do is try to think through the ways in which the non-Jewish partner can have an active role in raising the kids as Jews. The time of engagement is not too early to begin this conversation.

While Barbara needed to feel confident about John's commitment to help raise Jewish children, John needed to feel confident that Barbara recognized how difficult this decision was for him. He was fearful, and rightly so, about feeling like an outsider in relation to his own child. John vividly remembered the first family bar mitzvah he attended with Barbara. When he reached toward the yarmulkes, to put one on out of respect, one of Barbara's relatives quickly said, "Oh, you don't need one of those." As these words echoed in John's being, he wondered if it would ever be possible to be welcomed, to cease feeling like a total outsider. Barbara responded to John's concerns. Together, Barbara and John agreed to seek out a synagogue that welcomed interfaith couples. They both believed it would be the best way for everyone in the family to feel comfortable. John's fears were addressed, and as a family they found a religious home for themselves.

The third key for John and Barbara was being able to compromise. John put it this way:

> There will be a thousand issues that come up. You can agree to raise your kids Jewish, but what exact decisions you will make if it's a league championship game and Hebrew school on the same day are decisions you will make in the future. You will work through stuff as it comes up—both sides realizing that there will be differences and compromises along the way.

John and Barbara recognized that there is a contract, but the fine points of that contract, the thousand issues, will need constant renegotiating.

A year after their wedding, expecting their first child, John is still not sure why raising Jewish children is so important to Barbara. John still does not understand how Barbara can speak so passionately about tradition, about Jewish history, about Jewish social activism and philosophy and still choose not to participate regularly in home or synagogue rituals. Barbara admits that she cannot fully articulate why raising Jewish children is so dramatically important to her. She only knows that it is true for her, and she hopes to discover more reasons down the road. John ultimately accepts this because he loves her, and for this she is profoundly grateful. This then is the fourth key for interfaith relationships—like John and Barbara, you need to accept that religious feelings are complex and often defy rational and reasoned explanation. Also, they can change over time. Ultimately, it is vital for you to frequently check in with each other about your feelings and thoughts on religious matters.

One More Word about Children

You will, of course, have a variety of options to choose from regarding the religious upbringing of your children. They can be raised in the religion of one of the parents, with no religion, with pieces of both religions, or they can be exposed to various traditions, with an understanding that they will decide for themselves which religion, if any, they choose. Most clergy consider the first option most desirable. As rabbis, our preference would, of course, be for them to choose Judaism. However, what is more important is that parents make a clear choice to raise children in a particular religious tradition.

Identity formation is a complex process. Children feel safer and more comfortable with their own identities when their parents raise them in one religious tradition. While many similarities do exist among world religions, their theologies, worldviews, and understandings of humanity, just to name a few, differ radically. Also, their basic myths and stories teach different and often conflicting messages. As an adult, you may be able to sort through them. Children, on the other hand, hear the messages but are confused by what to make of them.

One family, trying to raise their children with both Judaism and Christianity, proudly told us how they put a dreidl on top of the Christmas tree every year, as a symbol of their commitment to both traditions. While an interesting picture, fusing the symbols neither honored nor respected either tradition. Another family chose to send their children to both church Sunday school and Hebrew school. When the third-grade Hebrew school teacher asked their son to tell everyone what he remembered about the story of Joseph, his inability to make sense of the two traditions became clear. He began with the story of Joseph and his brothers and the coat of many colors and then explained how, as an adult, Joseph served as the earthly father of Jesus. He knew two stories, of two very different Josephs, from two very different traditions.

The teacher did not know how to begin to respond to his answer. She reinforced the story of Joseph and his brothers and reoriented the rest of the class to the story they had been studying together. But she wanted to be sensitive to the way he was being raised and not dismiss the boy's father's religious tradition. So she began to explain that only Christians, not Jews, believed the second story that he told and that while both men were Josephs, they were not the same person. Religion and religious identity are highly complex. It is hard enough for an adult to gain an understanding and appreciation for multiple religious systems; it is far beyond most children's capabilities. Moreover, religious identity, as stated before, is often visceral, nonrational. It is taking as one's own a complex world of symbols and rituals.

Many parents who have attempted to let their children choose their religion when they reach a certain age find they have created an unanticipated problem: they have inadvertently put their children in a no-win situation. A large percentage of children raised in such households experience an unspoken tension; choosing religion, inadvertently and unexpectedly, becomes a matter of choosing one parent over the other. Imagine a ten-year-old choosing between *mommy's* Judaism and *daddy's* Christianity. Rarely can parents successfully keep emotional bonds and allegiances separate from the choice they place before their children.

Giving your children a religious heritage is giving them a gift. It is vital that you give your children consistent messages. This is precisely why the Reform Movement of Judaism enacted a policy in 1995 that children being raised in two religions should not attend Reform religious schools. Giving your children one religion is giving them the gift of identity, the gift of belonging to a community.

A final note: It is often said that it is easier to be in an intermarriage when one member of the couple is not involved in religion at all. From anecdotal evidence, this seems not to be the case. Non-identification or non-affiliation with a religious group does not necessarily reflect a person's allegiances or attitudes. Like Barbara and John, attendance and involvement can be deceptive. Also, implicit and explicit rejection of one's own religion can often manifest itself as an antipathy toward all organized religion, leaving little room for supporting a spouse or children in their religious practices.

These are complex issues, but they are not necessarily insurmountable. Remember, the keys to successfully navigating the waters of an interfaith relationship are: clarity, confidence, compromise, and a willingness to respond to change.

Rabbi, Will You Marry Us?

Barbara was bitter. She and John had spent a long time talking about what it meant to them to be in an interfaith relationship and how they would raise their kids. Now, they had gotten engaged, they had set a date, but they could not find a rabbi to marry them. First, she had called her family rabbi, the rabbi who had officiated at her bat mitzvah and confirmation, the rabbi who had done her grandmother's funeral. He had been happy to hear from her and genuinely pleased to hear that she was getting married. However, when she told him John wasn't Jewish, he said he could not perform the ceremony. She then called a number of other rabbis, only to find that the one who agreed to do it was charging an exorbitant sum of money. She was angry and disheartened. "Why," she asked, "is no rabbi willing to help us out, even though John has agreed to raise our children as Jews?"

The question of rabbinic participation in interfaith weddings is a source of heated debate within the liberal rabbinic community. Orthodox and Conservative rabbis are forbidden to perform them. The Reform Movement has an official position dissuading its rabbis from performing interfaith ceremonies; however, they are not barred from doing so. For Reform and Reconstructionist rabbis, the issue is a matter of personal and professional discretion and conscience. Some rabbis do not perform interfaith marriages because Jewish law has traditionally forbidden them. They believe that the marriage is invalid, Jewishly, if one of the partners is a non-Jew. They feel that the very marriage pledge, "Behold you are consecrated to me according to the laws of Moses and Israel," only has meaning when uttered by a Jew. Other rabbis who perform interfaith weddings do not share this view. They see the Jewish wedding ceremony as an evolving entity, whose language and symbols have been reinterpreted and changed through the centuries. They believe that Judaism's messages, even when expressed in a particularistic manner, can be meaningful for interfaith couples. Many also see performing an interfaith wedding as a way of welcoming non-Jews into the Jewish community and a way of keeping Jews within it as well. They believe that by doing interfaith ceremonies they increase the likelihood that the children will be raised as Jews. A small number of Jewish clergy are willing to co-officiate with clergy of other faiths.

The most important thing to remember if you find yourself frustrated that rabbis have turned you down is that it is nothing personal. Often couples perceive it as a personal rejection, as if the rabbi is *choos-*

ing not to perform *their* wedding. Most likely, though, the rabbi feels she or he *cannot* perform an interfaith marriage, no matter how compelling your situation.

After You Marry, Please Join

The Reform Movement has a clear policy that once an intermarriage has occurred, the couple should be welcomed into the community with open arms. This may seem hypocritical; as Barbara said, "One rabbi wouldn't have anything to do with marrying me, but said we'd be welcome as members. Why would I be a member of a community whose rabbi wouldn't marry me?" The answer is that while officiation reflects a rabbi's interpretation of Jewish law, communal membership is an option for all families with Jewish members. As one rabbi put it, "The best thing for the Jewish community, after the couple has gotten married, is to be open; you can hope that the family will raise the kids Jewish, and maybe even the non-Jewish partner will one day consider becoming Jewish."

Proposals: You Never Know

Most interfaith couples broach the subject of conversion at some point in their relationship. There are, generally speaking, three types of couples: those in which both members are observant adherents of different traditions; those in which one member will not marry unless there is a conversion; and those in which they speak of conversion, but make no decision. Those who fall into the last two categories have some interesting options. Kathy Kahn, Associate Director of the Outreach Department of the UAHC, explains conversion this way,

> Conversion to Judaism is like a marriage itself. Sometimes when an offer of marriage has been made, there might be some interest, but there might be some concern that for one reason or another it would not work out. If you have married someone Jewish— Judaism has made you a standing proposal. You may think about consecrating it now, or five years from now, but the proposal for marriage remains.

We encourage couples to explore the possibility of conversion. Many individuals worry about pushing their religion on to their partners. However, there is an important difference between pushing and proposing. Whether someone chooses to accept the proposal is ultimately the individual's decision, something one partner cannot force upon the other. In any case, it makes sense for both of you to explore learning about each other's traditions.

One never knows where this exploration will lead. Jack took an "Introduction to Judaism" class simply to learn more about Judaism, not to prepare for conversion. For the first eight weeks, he and Sharon came home from classes discussing the material. Then, after the ninth class, seemingly out of nowhere, Jack turned to Sharon and said, "I think I'm going to convert." "When did that happen?" Sharon asked. Jack paused and said, "It all just sort of fell together for me—it made sense."

Not every couple will find such a quick or easy resolution. Being an interfaith family is a challenging, but not impossible, proposition. With clarity, confidence, compromise, and a willingness to respond to changing perspectives on religious issues, your relationship can survive and flourish.

Exercise 42. Your Shared Religious History

Part I

Separately, answer the following questions. Then share your answers with each other.

1. When did you first realize you were of different religious backgrounds?
2. What was your first response when you found out?
3. Did it seem like an important issue to you from the start?

Part II

Separately, answer the following questions. Then share your answers with each other.

1. How connected to your religion do you see yourself as being?
2. What aspects of your religious tradition are central to your identity?
3. How is your religious identity tied to your sense of family? How does this relate to the holidays and other rituals you celebrate?
4. Can you imagine not participating in these family celebrations?
5. How connected to his/her religion do you see your partner as being?
6. What aspects of that religious tradition do you see as central to his/her identity?
7. How is his/her religious identity tied to his/her sense of family? How does this relate to the holidays and other rituals she/he celebrates?
8. Can you imagine your partner not participating in these family celebrations?

Part III

Separately, answer the following questions. Then share your answers with each other.

1. The first time you spent a holiday with your partner's family, how did you feel?
2. How do you feel now?
3. How do you relate to the celebrating that is happening?
4. How do you feel seeing your partner in that environment?
5. How welcome do you feel?
6. How comfortable are you participating in all that the family does?

Part IV

Separately, answer the following questions. Then share your answers with each other.

1. If family celebrations now take place in the home of someone in your parents' generation, would you eventually like to carry on the tradition in your own home? If so, how closely would you want your celebration to resemble theirs?

2. How comfortable would you be celebrating in your home the things that your in-laws celebrate in their home?

❧ Conditions and Promises: Religious Practices ❧

Articulate a few statements about the religious conditions you are depending on as you plan your wedding and anticipate your marriage. Articulate a few statements about the promises you will make to each other regarding your distinct religious traditions and practices and your expectations for raising children, if you plan to have them.

8

Spirituality: Asking Life's Big Questions

Soul Work

Dan was really surprised to hear Rachel say it. They had been together for a number of years and shared everything, he had thought. But then Rachel decided it was time to tell Dan that every night, before going to sleep, she prayed. Rachel prayed? He was stunned and filled with questions: "Right here, next to me? And, I never knew! What do you say? What do you think? Why do you pray?" Rachel, a bit uncomfortable, said to Dan, "It's not a big deal. My mother taught me how to say the *Sh'ma*, and I say it every night right before I close my eyes." Dan asked her why she had never told him this before. They had slept in the same bed on countless nights, and he had never noticed her doing it. Rachel responded, "Well, y'know." As she rolled over to go sleep, Rachel realized she was not exactly sure why she had never told Dan. Maybe she was embarrassed, or maybe she felt that it was one thing she wanted to keep just to herself. She'd never thought about it before. She did know that she'd never before felt a desire to share this with anyone. And now that she had, she was at a loss as to how to explain the power and meaning of this very personal daily ritual, even to the person she loved.

Every summer Rob went by himself to the mountains for ten days. Rick knew that Rob liked to go off by himself and never asked to go along with him. One year, as Rob was packing, Rick commented on the fact that Rob was going to get "his time away, to clear his head, to escape the world." Rob looked at him, realizing that Rick had come up with his own explanation of why he went away each year and that, in reality, it had little connection to his real reasons. Rob paused. Then he said, "Sit down. Let me explain. I don't go away to escape from the world. I go away to get reconnected, reacquainted with the world. I don't just clear my head. I fill it with the things that really matter. Nothing reminds me of how small I am, how insignificant my life and problems are in the grand scheme of things, than standing out in nature surrounded by towering mountains. There, more than anywhere else, I am reminded of how everything in the world is connected, how awesome and beautiful our planet is, and how grateful I am for my place in it." Rick was surprised. He had never heard Rob reflect in this way. He had had no idea that this was why Rob "headed for the hills" every year.

As Julie and Hank sat at an outdoor summer concert, Julie rested comfortably in Hank's arms. Gradually, he felt Julie's position shift. Her muscles got tighter, and her body started to quiver. Silently, she was gently crying. When Hank asked her why she was crying, she haltingly said she didn't know. A few minutes later, she said, "I've never heard anything so magnificently beautiful, so profoundly moving as the last few bars of that piece. It felt like everything, not just the disparate notes and instruments, but perhaps everything in the world could achieve that kind of resolution and harmony." Hank was taken aback by her words. He had thought it was beautiful, but she had heard it and experienced it on an entirely different level.

Marge volunteered every week at a soup kitchen. Gary thought it was really nice of her and always looked forward to hearing about her experiences. She clearly connected with the other volunteers and with the people whose meals she prepared and served. One night, Gary said, "I just don't know how you find the time. You're so busy. Yet, every week, barring some unforeseen emergency, you're there." Marge responded unself-consciously. "It may sound clichéd, but deep inside I feel it keeps me honest and aware, 'there but for the grace of God, go I.' I live such an incredibly blessed life; I can't just accept my blessings without giving something back." She paused for a minute and then continued. "My earliest memories are of my parents and grandparents volunteering, giving of their time and money. They said it was a 'Jewish' thing to do. They said, 'If you aren't a mensch, your life isn't worth living.' I guess their beliefs have become my own."

We are socialized not to share our spiritual lives and beliefs even with those with whom we are most intimate; in fact, most of us lack the language and tools to express the hows and whys of our spiritual feelings and practices. Many of us were raised to believe that only religious professionals and fanatics, or those out to proselytize, speak openly and frequently about religion and the soul. It is not uncommon for us, as rabbis, to be working with members of a couple who, after five, ten, fifteen years, are just learning about each other's spiritual practices and beliefs. It may be that one partner says a brief prayer every night before going to sleep or before getting on a plane. Or that he feels strongly attached to a particular religious practice or belief. Or that she ascribes importance or meaning to a particular action or ethic. Or that he understands the world in a particular way. Rarely do couples talk seriously and in depth about their beliefs, their reasons for engaging in religious or spiritual practices and rituals, and their connections with the religious or ethnic or national aspects of their identities. This is as true for couples who go to synagogue every Shabbat as it is for those who rarely or never go. Couples do not take the time to wrestle with and share their approaches to questions about their belief in God, their understandings about the meaning of life and death, or the place of spirituality in their lives.

Allowing another person to know about your spiritual life is a profound sign of trust and intimacy. To embark on a life journey with someone, not knowing how they find meaning in the world and in their own existence, can lead to unexpected conflicts, struggles, and confusions. In the following pages you will find texts, questions, and exercises designed to give some structure to your exploration of your fundamental beliefs, as a means to add depth to your relationship and figuratively unveil another part of the face of your beloved.

Jacob Saw Rachel

While he [Jacob] was still speaking with them [the shepherds], Rachel came with her father's flock; for she was a shepherdess. And when Jacob saw Rachel, the daughter of his uncle Laban, and the flock of his uncle Laban, Jacob went up and rolled the stone off the mouth of the well, and watered the flock of his uncle Laban. Then Jacob kissed Rachel and broke into tears.

Genesis 29:9–11

Traditionally, Jews have attempted to grapple with life's big questions by studying pieces of the Torah. First, details of the text are studied; then larger issues or issues not explicitly dealt with, but implicit in the text, are explored. The story of Jacob and Rachel's meeting, already mentioned in the first chapter, is rich with meanings and questions and will provide a paradigm for exploring spirituality. We begin by looking at the basic text.

Exercise 43: Experiences of Inspiration

Discuss the following initial questions about the text with your partner:

1. Seeing Rachel with her flock at the well led Jacob to roll the massive rock off the well to water the flock.
   a. What has moved you to take action, even when it has not been requested or expected?
   b. Can you explain why you responded as you did, what your motivation or inspiration was?
2. Jacob kissed Rachel and broke into tears.
   a. What moved Jacob to tears?
   b. What experiences in your life have moved you to tears—either tears of joy or sadness? Do you know what led you to be so profoundly touched and why tears emerged?

Jacob's removal of the rock from the well can be read on a few different levels. The Torah implies that it usually takes a number of men to lift a rock off a well, but Jacob did it by himself. On a simple level, perhaps Jacob, taken by Rachel, was trying to impress her with his physical prowess and generosity of spirit by rolling the rock off the well. He saw the pretty woman walking toward him, so he engaged in a macho physical act. On another level, his uncorking the contents of the well has a deep symbolism of its own.

From our previous discussions, we know the well is the central meeting place. However, the well was much more than that; it was also the source of life. For desert dwellers, a source of water was the difference between survival and death. When Jacob rolls the stone off the well, he is not simply providing physical life, he is symbolically opening up a well of love to nourish both of them. As a well of water gives physical sustenance, love gives spiritual sustenance, allowing for growth and vitality. Sharing your intimate thoughts and experiences deepens your relationship. Metaphorically, you are plumbing the depths of your wells together.

Exercise 44: Spirituality

Part I

Separately, take some time to answer the following questions:

1. How do you try to sustain and nurture your partner's spirituality?
2. How do you experience your partner trying to sustain and nurture your spirituality?
3. How have you grown since you met?
4. In what ways have you seen your partner grow since you met?
5. How do you express your joy and gratitude for having found each other?

Part II

Share and discuss your answers with each other.

Destiny and Bashert

Many couples speak of feeling that they were destined to meet, destined to be with each other. Somehow their meeting was part of a bigger plan. In Yiddish, the word for "destined" is *bashert.* So strong was the notion that one's mate was a matter of destiny that in Eastern Europe a fiancé/e was referred to as a *bashert/e,* much like the English "intended."

The most common way for Jews through the centuries to capture this sense of something being planned or ordained is to attribute it to God, the identified all-knowing Source of all. Curiously, God is never mentioned in the story of Jacob and Rachel. However, Jewish commentators saw God's presence, God's hand, in the story of their meeting and falling in love. *Zohar Chadash* 1:103 teaches that it was God who sent Rachel out to meet Jacob, since she was destined to become his mate.

In a midrash from the early medieval period, the well that Rachel and Jacob draw water from is referred to as a well filled with God's spirit (*B'reishit Rabbah* 70:9). *Zohar Chadash* 152 even claims that the waters of the well miraculously rose as a sign from God that Jacob should marry Rachel.

Centuries later, in the latter half of the nineteenth century, Y'hudah Aryeh Leib Alter of Ger, a Chasidic rabbi, looked for hidden meaning in the story of Jacob and Rachel by examining the language used in the narrative. He saw a link between the Hebrew verb *vayagel*, meaning "to roll [the rock off the well]," and the verb root *galah*, commonly meaning "a revelation of God." Therefore, he concluded, at the moment Jacob rolled the rock away and saw his future wife, he experienced God; God was revealed to him.

Exercise 45: A Spiritual Component

Discuss the following questions with your partner:

1. Would you characterize your meeting as having had a spiritual component?
2. Did you have an experience of something beyond just the two of you when you first met?
3. Did you think that God was present at your meeting?
4. Following the interpretation of the Y'hudah Aryeh Leib Alter, also known as the S'fat Emet, can you describe the moment when you had the revelation that your partner was "the one"?

Random or Ordained?

Previously, we discussed the role of the matchmaker in Jewish tradition. The ultimate matchmaker in Jewish tradition is God. A midrash says:

A person's marriage partner is from the Holy One. At times, a man is guided to his spouse's home; at other times, the spouse is guided to a man's home.

B'reishit Rabbah 68:3

Another midrash suggests that even before one is born, God has already designated a mate (BT *Sotah* 2a). For many, it may be difficult to believe in the literal meaning of God's preordaining your meeting. However, no matter where you met, at a bar or at a class, in cyberspace, through a friend, at a singles' event, or at work, Jewish tradition would still understand it as God's doing. In fact, Jewish tradition sees the work of bringing couples together as a special part of God's work.

A midrash recounts:

A Roman noblewoman asked Rabbi Yosei bar Chalafta, "How long did it take God to create the world?"

"Six days," he replied.

"And what has God been doing since then?" she asked.

"God pairs off people for marriage." Rabbi Yosei told her.

"Is this God's occupation?" she asked derisively, "I could do that too! I possess a great number of men servants and maid servants and would be able to pair all of them off in one hour!"

"You may think it is easy, but for God, it is as difficult as parting the Red Sea," he said.

After Rabbi Yosei left, the noblewoman formed rows of her men servants and her maid servants, a thousand in each row, and said to them, "This man shall marry this woman," pairing them off as she walked down the line for the night.

But when they returned to work the next morning, one had an injured head, one was missing an eye, and one had a broken foot.

"What is going on here?" the matron asked.

"I don't want this one [for a partner]," they all said.

She sent for Rabbi Yosei and told him, "There is no God like your God. When you explained to me that God is busy making matches, you spoke wisely."

B'reishit Rabbah 68:4

While it may be difficult for you to believe that your coming together was ordained by God, it may be equally difficult for you to believe that it was pure chance. Rabbi Lawrence Kushner puts it this way:

> When you first fell in love, confessed to each other that this romance must now build a home, there was a moment when you understood that the intention was not yours alone. There was a moment when to say anything less than that "since the creation of the universe it was written that that woman and this man would stand under this tree and agree to build a home together"—would be blasphemy.
>
> Lawrence Kushner,
> *Honey from the Rock*
> (Woodstock, Vt.: Jewish Lights, 1990)

Exercise 46. Random or Ordained?

Discuss the following questions with your partner:

1. How do you understand your finding each other? Was it *bashert?* Was it random?
2. Were you waiting for your partner to come into your life?
3. Have there been points in your relationship where you felt destiny to be at work?
4. In general, do you believe things happen because of destiny, a preordained plan?
   a. If yes, can you articulate some other times when you have felt this sense of destiny? Is this sense connected to a belief in God?
   b. If no, do you perceive the world as random or as having some kind of order?
5. Do you believe in miracles?

Eleazer's Prayer

Abraham sent Eleazer on a mission to find a mate for his son Isaac. Eleazer understood the import of his master's request and was fearful that he would not be able to fulfill it. At the well, Eleazer paused and prayed:

"Adonai, God of my master Abraham, grant me good fortune this day, and deal graciously with my master Abraham: Here I stand by the spring as the daughters of the townsmen come out to draw water; let the maiden to whom I say, 'Please, lower your jar that I may drink,' and who replies, 'Drink, and I will also water your camels,' let her be the one whom You have decreed for Your servant Isaac. Thereby shall I know that You have dealt graciously with my master."

Genesis 24:12–14

From time immemorial, human beings have been moved to pray for things they want and need—out of a sense of wonder and gratitude, in an effort to be forgiven; and for guidance. Each organized religious group has its own normative and fixed styles of worship and prayer. For some people, these inform the ways in which they express their deepest responses to the world in which they live. Other people find themselves spontaneously and fluidly experiencing a sense of wonder or gratitude, a sense of remorse or desire, and find themselves articulating those feelings in a less formal, yet still conscious manner.

Exercise 47. Moments of Conscious Connection

Part I

Separately, answer the following questions:

1. When was the last time you were awed by something in the natural world?
    a. How did you become aware of it?
    b. What sensations did it evoke in you?
    c. What thoughts did it engender in you?
    d. Did you share the moment and your responses to it with anyone else?
        1. If so, why did you choose to do so?
        2. If not, do you understand why you didn't?
    e. Were you moved to verbally respond to the moment?
    f. Did you understand it then, or now, as a spiritual or religious moment?

2. Does your partner share these experiences with you or anyone else?
3. How does your partner's spirituality affect your relationship?
   a. Does it enhance it?
   b. Does it detract from it?

Part II

Discuss your responses with each other.

There is a Chasidic saying that a *tzaddik*, a righteous person, should never remain stagnant, but should always be reaching for the next level of spiritual development. As individuals and as a couple, continual spiritual growth is vital to your development. There might be certain spiritual disciplines that you already practice—prayer, Torah study, meditation, running—and there might be certain practices that you wish to develop. Encouraging each other to maintain or develop such practices will be crucial to maintaining balance in life.

Some couples set aside time each week for Torah study; some couples set aside time each year to go on a meditation or yoga retreat. Some couples do these activities apart, allowing each other to pursue those things they find most meaningful. Kathy goes away for two weeks every year to a retreat center before the High Holy Days, while Bill takes care of the kids and the home. They have been doing this for years. Bill says, "It's incredibly important for her to renew herself each year, and I want to give her that opportunity." David goes to synagogue every Saturday morning, while Jen stays at home and reads. At first this annoyed both of them. Jen wanted David to stay home and be with her on one of their rare days off, and David wanted Jen to go to synagogue with him. But they both realized that they needed to be supportive of the other's needs. Finding a balance may be more difficult and challenging than it appears. It is often easy to think that your world would be perfect if only your partner shared all of your interests. You will probably be happiest if you do share some interests. But honoring and encouraging your different needs and desires will also contribute to your happiness and enrich your lives. For some couples, it is a fine line to walk.

✒ Conditions and Promises: Soul Work ✒

Produce statements that capture the spiritual growth, or soul work, that you will try to promote and support for each other and with each other.

Life's Ups and Downs: Coping with Adversity and Loss

Jacob and Rachel after the Well: Life's Highs and Lows

The first time Jacob and Rachel met, Jacob cried and he kissed her. He knew he had found his *basherte*. However, theirs is not a story of immediate gratification. Rather, Jacob agreed to work for seven years for Rachel's father, Laban, at the end of which he was promised to have Rachel as his bride. Jacob worked those seven years but was then tricked by Laban into marrying Rachel's older sister, Leah. Jacob had to agree to work for another seven years in exchange for marrying Rachel. The story of love at first sight became one of jealousy and struggle as Jacob, Leah, and Rachel negotiated their complicated relationships.

Maintaining a sense of euphoria and gratitude is often a painful and difficult struggle. Jacob and Rachel struggled to do it. After God parted the Reed Sea, the Israelites marched through it, celebrating and praising God for their newfound safety. However, they soon began to complain bitterly to God, questioning why they were taken out of Egypt to wander in the desert. Their faith was seriously shaken. Their initial euphoria and sense of gratitude were quickly replaced with bitterness and struggle.

The Torah teaches that moving between praise and gratitude and confusion and struggle is part of life. Most people who describe themselves as having faith have been through periods of frustration, conflict, and confusion. Often through those times, more so than in times of ease and comfort, we forge enduring beliefs and understandings. Exploring how you deal with adversity, disappointment, and loss—as individuals and as a couple—can deepen your understanding of yourselves and can help you see ways you can best support each other.

Exercise 48: Adversity and Coping

Part I

Separately, answer the following questions:

1. What points in your life do you feel were the biggest struggle?
2. How did you respond to them? What did you turn to: beliefs, practices, places, people, etc.?
   a. If you turned to other people:
      1. To whom did you turn and why?
      2. Did they provide you with what you needed?
   b. If you did not turn to others:
      1. Why did you make this choice?
      2. What *did* you turn to?
   c. If in the same circumstances again, would you want to change your response?
      1. If so, how?
      2. If not, why?
3. What lasting impact do you believe those times have had on you, your sense of self, and your sense of faith?

Part II

Share and discuss your answers with your partner.

Love and Loss

Jewish commentators, looking at the story of Jacob's meeting Rachel, were moved by the remark about Jacob's tears. Why did Jacob cry at the moment he saw his beloved for the first time? Perhaps he was overcome by the emotion of the moment; he felt passion, joy, and expectation, so he cried. Rashi, however, explains Jacob's crying as his response to a premonition that his beloved Rachel would die before he did. Why would Rashi bring up death at the moment of lovers first meeting? Marriage and loss are intertwined in an almost inexplicable way. Somehow the magnitude of finding a life partner transforms some people's understanding of loss and even death.

With every life transition, every movement along the life cycle, there is change and loss. Engagements and marriage are cause for joy and celebration. They also underscore the passage of the years. Relationships between parents and children change with engagement and marriage. Something of the earlier relationship is lost. Consider the fact that as you prepare to become each other's life partners, changing your status to that of a married couple, so, too, the status of every other member of your families is changing. While this may be, from everyone's vantage point, for the better, it is a transition with profound effects. The tears shed at your wedding, by you and by others, are likely to be bittersweet, as people imagine the joy of your future and grapple with how much has changed.

Jewish tradition makes this link explicit through a number of rituals connected with marriage. In some profound way, we can gain a deeper appreciation of life's fragility and the impact of the passage of time at the very moment we enter into life's most tender and enduring relationships. As you will see in chapter 9, the *t'nai-im* ceremony enables future mothers-in-law to assert their new status, while affirming their continued commitment to protecting their children.

Exercise 49. Life's Transitions and Loss

Share your thoughts about the following with each other:

1. The losses you are experiencing as you anticipate marriage.
2. The losses your parents, siblings, and grandparents might be experiencing as they anticipate your marriage.
3. Ways in which you might be sensitive to or respond to these losses, for each other and for others.

Loss and Death

Discussing loss and death, our responses to them, our experiences with them, and our understandings of them, is never easy. Contemplating death, our own and that of others, is scary. You and your partner may already have lived through the loss of a significant person in your lives. If not, you can only imagine what such an experience will be like. Your understanding about death and mourning is intimately related to your understanding of life and its meaning. Though difficult, we encourage you to take time to work through these exercises.

Exercise 50. Death and Life

Part I

Discuss your answers to the following questions with each other:

1. Do you believe the following words?

   To everything there is a season and a time for every purpose under heaven. A time to be born, a time to die.

   Ecclesiastes 3:1–2

2. Do we know when those times will be?
3. Do we have a right to control either of them?
   a. If so, what gives us that right, and are there any limits attached to that right?
   b. If not, why not? Are they controlled by anyone or anything?
4. How do you feel about living wills?
5. Do you have a lawyer to consult about these matters?

Part II

Discuss your family's mourning patterns with your partner.

1. Did your family have "right and appropriate" ways to mourn and grieve? What were/are they?
2. As an adult, have you continued these ways, or have you found new ones?

Part III

Discuss the following questions with each other:

1. Were you raised in a family where people had wills and cemetery plots?
2. Do you anticipate following that pattern?

Exercise 51. "Whither Thou Goest, I Will Go. . . Where Thou Diest, I Will Die"

"Do not entreat me to leave you . . . for wherever you go, I will go; and wherever you lodge, I will lodge; your people shall be my people; and your God, my God; where you die, I will die, and there will I be buried."

Ruth 1:16–17

These famous biblical words uttered by Ruth reflect expectations that many couples have when they enter marriage. They will travel through life side by side, and in death, they will be buried side by side. Your attitudes about life are intimately tied to your perspectives and beliefs about death. Therefore, as you contemplate the ways that making an enduring commitment to each other will alter your lives, sharing your understanding about death, dying, and mourning can deepen your relationship. Some couples find it easier to have these discussions with a rabbi or cantor as a facilitator.

Discuss the following questions with each other:

1. What are your expectations at death?
    a. Will you be buried, cremated, etc.?
    b. Will there be a funeral?
        1. If so, will it follow a specific religious tradition?
        2. If not, what arrangements would you like to be made?
2. If you will be buried, where do you expect to be buried?
    a. In a family plot?
    b. In whose family plot?

Exercise 52. The Here and the Hereafter

A midrash tells us:
> The day of death is when two worlds meet and kiss; this world going out and the future world coming in.
>
> JT *Y'vamot* 15:2

Discuss the following questions with each other:

1. How do you understand death? Is it a harbor, a haven of rest, nothingness, bliss, etc.?
2. Do you know what has influenced your notions about death?
3. What are your beliefs pertaining to life after death?

✺ Conditions and Promises: Planning for Death ✺

Try to write a few statements that clearly reflect your expectations (conditions) regarding wills, death, and burial and the types of promises you are willing to make to each other related to them.

Rituals

9

T'nai-im Ceremonies:
Renewing the Jewish Engagement Party

Josh and Leah stared at each other nervously. It was four months before their wedding, and 100 rejoicing relatives and friends stood around them expectantly watching their every move. As Leah picked up the pen on the table in front of them, the crowd slowly began to sing Jewish wedding songs. Amidst the joyous choruses, Josh and Leah signed a document, handed each other a shekel (an Israeli coin), announced their love and desire to marry each other, and joined with everyone in shouting "Mazal tov!" as Leah's mother smashed a plate.

Josh and Leah chose to renew a custom that has for the most part been lost to modern Jews: a *t'nai-im* ceremony. Josh said:

> When we got engaged, it seemed like we spent a lot of time worrying about tablecloths and flowers. Talking about what it really meant to be engaged fell through the cracks. But having this ceremony in front of friends and family really strengthened our sense of commitment to each other.

Traditionally, Jews marked and celebrated an engagement at a *t'nai-im* ceremony. There, the rabbi shared the conditions and agreements made by the families of the bride and groom with the community and announced the betrothal and the date of the wedding. When Josh and Leah wanted to find a uniquely Jewish way to celebrate their engagement, they decided that the *t'nai-im* ceremony would serve as a wonderful bridge to their wedding. Their engagement party turned into something much more meaningful than just a large dinner with friends and relatives. Josh reflected:

I believe that everyone present felt as if they had been part of something special by witnessing our *t'nai-im* ceremony. Together we all shared the intimacy of a powerful moment.

Aaron and Jodi had a *t'nai-im* ceremony a few months before their wedding. For Aaron the ceremony became more than he could have anticipated:

I was transformed by the whole experience. The very nature of my relationship with Jodi had reached a new plane of existence. Our relationship had taken on a different level of seriousness and permanence. I looked at her differently. I felt a strong sense of commitment—a sense of there's no turning back. The moment was so transformative that it had to be holy.

Maya and Kari read the words articulating their hopes and commitments to each other aloud and in unison, as a small group of intimate friends listened attentively. As they finished reading, they handed the document to their friends to sign. Then, they signed it themselves. As Maya said:

It's one thing to tell the person you love that you plan to be there for years to come, that you will do everything in your power to help the relationship grow and mature. It's another to read those words and share those pledges with other people, particularly the people who will help you follow through with your promises.

For Josh and Leah, Aaron and Jodi, and Maya and Kari, having a *t'nai-im* ceremony forced them to think about their commitment to each other and what they hoped their relationship would become. Their love of Judaism served as a catalyst for them to use a ritual with roots that go back deep into the Jewish soul.

What Is a T'nai-im *Ceremony?*

Like many Jewish rituals, the *t'nai-im* ceremony has largely fallen out of use, except in some Orthodox circles, where a version of the traditional ceremony is performed right before the wedding. However, a growing, but still small number of liberal Jews are renewing and redefining this ritual. At its most basic, the *t'nai-im* ceremony is a betrothal ritual. It consists of preparing and signing a special document, which enumerates certain conditions for the wedding, and reciting some blessings. Yet, Jewish communities around the world and in different historical circumstances have found ways to expand what once was a legal ritual into a celebratory one.

The word *t'nai-im* literally means "conditions." It refers to a document known as the *t'na-ei rishonim* (first conditions), but more popularly known by its shorthand *t'nai-im*. The *t'nai-im* is called the first conditions because on the day of the wedding, the couple signs the more well-known wedding document, the *ketubah*, which is also known as the *t'na-ei acharonim* (later conditions). The conditions set forth in the *ketubah* take the place of the *t'nai-im*.

The *t'nai-im* document was signed when two families had agreed that their children should marry. The betrothal document stipulated the conditions that the families agreed upon for marriage, which traditionally included each family's commitments regarding dowry, gifts to be given between bride and groom, responsibility for wedding expenses, and the date and place of the wedding. Also stipulated in the document was a penalty to be paid if the engagement was broken.

The *t'nai-im* document was initially used in the Middle Ages, but its roots go back to the Talmud (approximately 400–600 C.E.) Signing a *t'nai-im* document was taken as seriously as the wedding itself. Given the pain and confusion engendered by a broken engagement, the Gaon of Vilna, a renowned eighteenth-century rabbi, went so far as to advise a betrothed male to marry his fiancée and get a divorce, rather than break the *t'nai-im* document and pay the penalty. (For further information about the history of the *t'nai-im* ceremony, see appendix 2.)

An Old Custom for New Times

The revival of the *t'nai-im* ceremony as an actual engagement ceremony reflects the desire of some Jews today to relate to and engage with Jewish rituals and customs in meaningful ways. Rather than create from scratch, many people look back to traditional customs and observances to gain both an appreciation for what has existed and to develop new and creative ways to find personal and enduring values in either their form, content, or message. This often means rejecting some of the language and values of our ancestors, while simultaneously infusing our inherited tradition with a more modern sensibility.

The *t'nai-im* ceremony can be an opportunity to reflect upon and internalize the profound personal changes you are experiencing as individuals and as members of the couple. Josh said:

> The engagement is a difficult time. I didn't really know what it meant to be engaged. It was like it had no status, all you had to show for it was this ring, but with the document and the ceremony, you're sort of branded—wow, you are engaged.

Having a *t'nai-im* ceremony can also provide you and those present with an opportunity to understand the depth and meaning of your commitment to each other. As Aaron said right after his *t'nai-im:*

> By having a ceremony in front of friends and family, you know you made a commitment. Something had happened.

Another psychological benefit that some couples experience as a result of planning and celebrating a *t'nai-im* ceremony is that it becomes the locus for some of the tensions and serves as a valve for releasing them. During this time of transition from single to married, you and the members of your family of origin are likely to struggle and experience tensions as you renegotiate your relationships. For many people, the impact of these changing family dynamics rises to the surface and gets expressed in both direct and indirect ways as the details of the wedding are negotiated. This tension is often worked out over the details of the wedding. Reminding yourselves and others of your reasons for wanting to marry can help everyone refocus attention from the mundane matters of the wedding plans to the reasons the two of you want to spend your life together. Some couples also find that by having the *t'nai-im* ceremony, they are able to handle the wedding negotiations much more easily. The *t'nai-im* ceremony helps everyone return to the big picture.

Reasons for choosing to have a *t'nai-im* ceremony are varied. Aaron and Jodi were going to use a traditional *ketubah* for their wedding, but they struggled with its patriarchal language and sought a way to articulate their own feelings about their relationship. The *t'nai-im* document gave them an opportunity to creatively express themselves and their commitments. Maya and Kari had a *t'nai-im* ceremony because they knew that during their engagement period they were going to be separated for a long time. By having a *t'nai-im* ceremony, they felt their status as an engaged couple was affirmed. It provided them with a greater sense of security. The *t'nai-im* ceremony served its traditional purpose of solidifying the agreement to marry.

Creating Contemporary *T'nai-im* Ceremonies

Jews are known as the People of the Book for a good reason. We are a people bound to the written word. So central is the written word that at the core of two of life's most important ceremonies, we read a document aloud: the *ketubah* at a wedding and the *t'nai-im* document at an engagement ceremony.

In creating a contemporary *t'nai-im* ceremony, the first step is to decide which type of text you would like to use: the traditional document, a version that combines traditional and creative elements, or one entirely of your own creation. If you choose the traditional document, your only job is to find a person qualified to fill in the specific details correctly. You can find preprinted versions, engage a calligrapher, or prepare it on a computer. For many couples, however, the importance of the document lies in the opportunity to be creative and to use the *t'nai-im* document to think about what it means to be engaged.

The Document

The Traditional Document

The traditional *t'nai-im* document uses legal terminology and is focused on monetary and material concerns. It is written in Aramaic, the lingua franca of Jewish legal transactions. Many *t'nai-im* documents now also include a translation into the vernacular of the country in which Jews reside. The document announces an engagement in a highly formulaic and legalistic manner. If this surprises you, remember that for most of Jewish history, weddings were primarily financial, not romantic, agreements made between two families.

The Traditional *T'nai-im* Document

To a Good Fortune

May it come up and sprout forth like a green garden. One who finds a wife, finds goodness, and obtains favor of the good Lord, who consecrates this union.

May He who predestinates, bestow a good name and future to the provisions embodied in this agreement, which were agreed upon by the two parties hereto, that is, as party of the first part, Mr. _____, who represents the groom, Mr. _____, and as party of the second part, Mr. _____, who represents the bride, Miss _____.

Firstly: That the above named groom agrees to take to himself as wife the above named bride, through *chuppah* and betrothal, in accordance with the law of Moses and Israel; that they will neither abstract nor conceal from one another any property whatsoever, but they shall equally have power over their property, pursuant to the established custom.

The above named groom obligates himself to present the bride gifts according to custom.

The above named bride obligates herself to give as her dowry the sum of _____, in cash, and clothes, and pillows and linens, as is the custom.

The wedding will take place, if the Almighty so wills it, on the _____ day of _____ in the year _____ or sooner or later than that date if both sides agree to it.

A fine is to be paid by the party breaking this agreement, to the other party, in the fixed sum of _____, and also in accordance with the law of the land.

All of the foregoing was done with perfect understanding and due deliberation, and by means of the most effective method, in accordance with the ordinance of the Sages, of blessed memory, and in accordance with the law of the land; by means of striking hands, by solemn promises, by true affirmation, by handing over an object (from one party to the other), to take effect immediately; and this is not to be regarded as a mere forfeiture without consideration, or as a mere formula of a document. We have followed the legal formality of *kinyan* (symbolic acquisition), by handing over an object, between the groom and the bride and their representatives, by using a garment legally fit for the purpose, to validate all that is stated above.

And Everything Is Valid and Confirmed

For the further purpose of making this agreement binding and obligatory, the groom and the bride themselves have attached their signatures hereunto this ___ day of ___, in the year _____ at _____ [name of town].

Attested to: _____ (groom)
Attested to: _____ (bride)

In our presence, the undersigned witnesses, did the above named groom and bride attach their signatures, to affirm all that is stated above, and in our presence did they go through the legal formality of symbolical delivery, by handing over an object from one party to the other *(kinyan)*, that this agreement take effect immediately; and we have verified and affirmed it as is required by law.

In witness whereof, we have hereunto set our hands this _____ day of ____, in the year _____ at _____ [name of town].

Attested to: _____ (witness)
Attested to: _____ (witness)

Creating a Modern Document

If you choose to try creating a *t'nai-im* document, starting from scratch may be difficult or even daunting for you. Below you will find two things that might help get you started. First, you will find the traditional *t'nai-im* document broken down into its essential building blocks of content and meaning. Second, you will find examples of possible alternatives to use for each rubric.

Rubrics of the Traditional T'nai-im

You may want to refer back to the traditional document as you are looking at the following list of the rubrics of the traditional *t'nai-im*.

Recognition of Joy

At the top of the document is the phrase *Mazal Tov* (To a Good Fortune). This phrase is traditionally printed at the top of the *t'nai-im* document.

An Introductory Quote

The most common traditional quote, drawn in part from Proverbs 18:22, speaks of fertility and a man's good fortune in finding a wife:

> May it come up and sprout forth like a green garden. One who finds a wife, finds goodness, and obtains favor of the good Lord, who consecrates this union.

You may choose any quote that you feel captures your experience of what it has been like to find each other and what hopes have sprouted as a result of your meeting. Some quotes that others have put into their creative *t'nai-im* documents are:

> Let it sprout and grow as a well-watered garden. One who finds the right woman or man finds goodness. God's power will grant them goodness, and God will bless this union as good.
> Rabbi Michelle Missaghieh and Bruce Ellman

> You have created joy and gladness, bridegroom and bride, mirth and exaltation, pleasure and delight, love and harmony, peace and companionship.
> Traditional Jewish wedding blessing

> I am my beloved's and my beloved is mine.
> Song of Songs 2:16

> From every human being there rises a light that reaches straight to the heavens. When two souls that are destined to be together

find each other, their streams of light flow together and a single
brighter light goes forth from their united being.

Baal Shem Tov

God creates new worlds constantly by causing marriages to take
place.

Zohar 1:89a

Winter has passed, the rains have fled the earth and left it bright
    with blossoms.
Birds wing in the low sky, dove and songbird singing in the open
    air above.
Earth nourishing tree and vine, green fig and tender grape, green
    and tender fragrance.
Come with me, my love, come away.

Song of Songs 2:11–13

Representatives of the Bride and the Groom

As mentioned before, the original *t'nai-im* document confirmed a set of
financial obligations made between the families of the bride and groom,
often through legally appointed representatives. The parents or friends
of the family would act as the representatives.

The Details of the Wedding

Originally, the traditional *t'nai-im* document contained the name of the
bride and the groom, and the agreed upon time and place of the wedding. Over time, in response to the unpredictability of circumstances,
some communities adopted a custom of not specifying the exact date or
place, but merely writing the words, as agreed upon.

Consider how much detail you want to include about these things.
You may want to celebrate your engagement long before you have
worked out the details of your wedding. If you will consider this document as a binding document, will its validity be compromised if, due to
unforeseen circumstances, you are unable to meet every detail you
include? Or do you both understand some of these details as expectations rather than promises?

Gifts from the Groom to the Bride
and the Dowry from the Bride's Family

Historically, one of the ways that things of value passed from one family to another and from one generation to another was through the institution of marriage. Both families stood to gain from the match brokered for their children. Bride and groom, through their families' holdings or through the groom's earnings, were expected to provide each other with gifts that represented a pledge for the future. The form and value of the gifts was traditionally stipulated in the *t'nai-im*. If the gifts were not forthcoming, the engagement was not valid. In modernity, the most common pledge or gift is, of course, the engagement ring.

Traditionally, a bride's family had to take some responsibility for providing for their daughter's and son-in-law's financial well-being. The *t'nai-im* stipulated the size and content of the dowry a woman would bring into her marriage. In some communities, the dowry list included every article of clothing, every piece of linen and china. Literally everything the bride had of value was part of the dowry. Different parts of the dowry were subject to different laws of dispersal in the event of a divorce.

In Jewish communities around the world, an interesting alliance arose. In essence, Jewish communities had two criteria for determining their elite. The first was scholarship and learning. The second was wealth. For many centuries, scholarly families sought wealthy women to marry their sons, and wealthy families sought to enhance their prestige by becoming relatives of the learned class. It was considered a privilege for the bride's family to support their new son-in-law while he pursued his studies.

In a traditional *t'nai-im* document there is still a place for gifts and dowry. Interestingly, while the forms may be foreign, given the fact that each of you is entering your marriage with certain assets or liabilities and with certain expectations regarding your financial future, some contemporary *t'nai-im* documents have included detailed financial information in this section. In other documents, instead of a family dowry, the members of the couple have chosen to give each other gifts. The gifts given to each other might be listed in the *t'nai-im* document or actually given at the ceremony. Josh and Leah gave each other one shekel (Israeli currency) as symbolic gifts. Michelle and Bruce gave each other candlesticks and *tallitot* (prayer shawls), Jewish ritual objects they would use individually and during their regular religious celebrations. You might consider making a gift of *tzedakah* and writing that in the *t'nai-im*. You might also consider a nontangible gift such as a blessing to be given one to the other. Michelle and Bruce also listed the gifts from the heart that they each brought into the relationship, such as sensitivity, honesty, and inner strength.

The Penalty

Traditionally, the *t'nai-im* document was a recognized legal document. As such, it included information about penalties to be paid in case of a breach of contract. In this case a broken contract meant a broken engagement. The penalty, or *knas* in Yiddish, was historically one of the most important elements of the *t'nai-im* document, serving as insurance that both parties intended to uphold the agreement and celebrate the marriage.

Some couples reject the idea of a penalty in their *t'nai-im* and do not include any clause of this kind. Some set the amount at a symbolic level, like a penny or a trillion dollars. In Josh and Leah's *t'nai-im* however, they set a realistic amount of money as their penalty, 3,000 shekels, equivalent at that time to approximately $1,500. Because the *t'nai-im* is a document signed by witnesses, and because they used a realistic amount of money, their document might have been considered in many states a legally binding agreement. Leah had researched the matter and fully intended to make it legally binding. She said, "It was important for our relationship at the time that the *t'nai-im* be taken seriously and have real-life implications." Further, the couple and their families had spent a good deal of money on rings, a wedding hall, a wedding dress, a suit, and so on. For one of them to break off the engagement would really have caused the other financial harm.

Craig and Lori took the idea of the penalty in a completely different direction. They understood that the original intent of the penalty was to compel parties to go through with the wedding. Instead of a monetary penalty as an impetus to get married, they pledged to undertake a process of introspection and counseling if one of them felt a desire to back out. Their *t'nai-im* document reads, "If either one of us should consider breaking our engagement, a three-part process of evaluation should be undertaken including personal introspection, an honest and open discussion of our concerns, and counseling with a skilled professional."

Kinyan

Traditionally, legal acquisition, *kinyan*, is affirmed through three means: a written document, the transfer of property, and the transfer of money. For someone to take ownership of an object, he/she must do something to indicate his/her acceptance of it. At the time of betrothal, a symbolic acquisition takes place. Traditionally, *kinyan* can be affected in many ways, but the most commonly used method at an engagement or wedding is called *kinyan sudar*. This entails a person holding one end of a handkerchief and presenting the other end to each member of the couple (traditionally, only a man would do *kinyan*). The grabbing of the handkerchief signifies acceptance of the *t'nai-im* document. In effect, it is Jewish law's equivalent to signing your name, signifying that you consider everything that has transpired legal and valid.

Many contemporary liberal couples modify this part of the ceremony. They wish to affirm their mutual acceptance of the document and wish both partners to be equal and active participants. Some people have a designated person hold one end of the handkerchief and present the other end to both members of the couple.

Signatures of Witnesses, the Bride, and the Groom

According to Jewish law, two kosher male Jewish witnesses are needed to make the document valid. If you have questions about this for the validity of your document, consult a rabbi or someone else knowledgeable in halachah, Jewish law.

The liberal movements of Judaism recognize male or female signators as valid witnesses. Michelle and Bruce, for example, invited their parents and all of their guests to sign the document at their *t'nai-im* ceremony.

Modern *T'nai-im* Documents

Tradition with a Twist

Included here are two examples of *t'nai-im* documents that meld traditional elements and creative alternatives. Josh and Leah's, while very traditional, uses egalitarian forms and language. Bruce and Michelle's, on the other hand, freely utilizes traditional and alternative elements.

T'nai-im of Josh Caruso and Leah Weiss Caruso

May God who predestinates bestow a good name and future to the provisions embodied in this agreement, which were agreed upon by the two parties hereto, that is, as a party of the first part, Baht Yameen Weiss, who represents the groom, Josh Caruso, and the party of the second part, Dr. Phillip Weiss, who represents the bride, Leah Rachel Weiss.

Firstly: That the above named groom agrees to take to himself as wife the above named bride through *chuppah* and betrothal, in accordance with the laws of Moses and Israel. The above named bride agrees to take to herself as husband the above named groom, through *chuppah* and betrothal in the eyes of the people of Israel; that they will neither abstract nor conceal from one another any property whatsoever, but they shall equally have power over their property pursuant to the established custom.

The above named bride and groom obligate themselves to present each other with gifts according to custom, and as dowry the sum of one shekel in cash.

The wedding will take place, with the will of God on the seventh day of July in the year 1996 or sooner than such date or later if both parties agree thereto.

A fine is to be paid by the party breaking this agreement in the fixed sum of three thousand shekels, and also in accordance with the law of the land.

All of the foregoing was done with perfect understanding and due deliberations and by means of the most effective method, in accordance with the ordinance of the Sages of blessed memory, in accordance with the law of the land; by means of striking hands, by solemn promises, by true affirmation, by handing over an object between parties, to take effect immediately, that is not to be regarded as a mere forfeiture, without consideration or as a mere formula of a document. We have followed the legal formality of a *kinyan*, by handing over an object between the groom and the bride and their representatives by using a garment legally fit for this purpose to validate all that is stated above. And everything is valid and confirmed. For the further purpose of making this agreement binding and obligatory, the groom and the bride themselves have attached their signatures hereunto this thirteenth day of March in the year 1996 in Manhattan, New York.

Attested to: Josh Caruso   The Groom
Attested to: Leah Weiss   The Bride

In our presence, the undersigned witnesses, did the above named groom and bride attach their signatures to affirm all that is stated above, and in our presence did they go through the legal formality of *kinyan*, by handing over an object from one party to the other, that this agreement take effect immediately and we have verified and affirmed as is required by law. In witness whereof, we have hereunto set our hands this thirteenth day of March in the year 1996 in Manhattan, New York.

Attested to: [Various friends]   Witnesses

T'nai-im of Bruce Ellman and Michelle Missaghieh

Let it sprout and grow as a well-watered garden. One who finds the right woman or man finds goodness. God's power will grant them goodness, and God will bless this union as good.

May the One who speaks the past and the future, bestow a good name and future upon the words of this betrothal and its provisions, which were agreed upon by the two parties listed here on behalf of the bride and groom—the first party, Lavea Brachman, who stands to represent the groom Bruce Philip Ellman, and the second party, Barbara Zakin, who stands to represent the bride Michelle Paree Missaghieh.

Firstly, the above named groom agrees to marry as wife the above named bride and the above named bride agrees to marry the above named groom, through *chuppah* and *kiddushin* according to the laws of Moses and Israel. They will neither flee from nor conceal from one another any property whatsoever. Rather they shall equally have power over each other's estate according to the local custom.

The above named groom vows to present the bride with gifts according to custom. The above named bride vows to present the groom with gifts according to custom. Some gifts can be held in the hand and others in the heart. The former gifts will be candlesticks to celebrate the holidays and a tallit for prayer and learning, respectively. Both these gifts will bring light into their lives as it says: "God said, 'Let there be light,' and there was light" (Genesis 1:3) and "You, *Adonai*, are clothed in glory and majesty; wrapped in a robe of light" (Psalm 104:1–2).

The latter gifts come from the heart. The groom brings to the marriage insight, patience, kindness, sensitivity, hunger, and the desire for growth. The bride brings vision, determination, discipline, inner strength, honesty, love of the arts, and a passion for learning. Together they offer humor, family and community, intelligence and appreciation of the aesthetic, compassion and a commitment to Jewish values and observance.

The wedding will take place with *mazal tov* and God's will on the 13th day of Sivan 5758 corresponding to the 7th of June 1998, or before that date or after that date, with the consent of both parties.

If either party is stirred to consider the possibility of breaking this agreement, a process of personal introspection is first required. Then an open discussion of each party's concerns must take place between the bride and the groom. Lastly, the couple is obligated to work with a skilled counselor before a decision is reached.

All that is written above was done with full understanding and deliberation, with mutual respect, the spirit of our blessed Sages and the law of the land. By means of a handshake, sincere words, and *kinyan*. This agreement takes effect immediately, and is not to be regarded as a meaningless act. We have done *kinyan* from the groom and the bride and their representatives and all who witnessed the document by using a garment legally fit for *kinyan* to validate what is written above.

Everything Is Knotted and Exists

To further seal this agreement, the groom and the bride themselves sign on the eve of Rosh Chodesh Kislev 5758, which corresponds to the 29th of November 1997 in Columbus, Ohio.

Groom: Bruce Ellman
Bride: Michelle Missaghieh

In the presence of the undersigned witnesses, the groom and the bride named above attach their signatures to affirm all that is stated above. In addition they did *kinyan* in our presence in order for this agreement to take place immediately. We have verified and confirmed as is required by tradition and have signed below to prove this as a legal agreement on the eve of Rosh Chodesh Kislev, which corresponds to the 29th of November 1997.

Witnesses:

In addition we invite the parents of the groom and the bride to sign this document of betrothal as well as all present guests.

Parents of the Groom:
Parents of the Bride:
Guests:

Putting a Piece of Your Soul in It

Some couples have chosen to take the entire *t'nai-im* document in a new direction. Focusing on the meaning of the word *t'nai-im*, "conditions," they use the document to express the conditions upon which their relationship stands. In the document they stipulate the promises and conditions that they agree must be present if they are to marry.

For some couples who have chosen to renew the *t'nai-im* ceremony, writing their own *t'nai-im* has proved the most valuable part of the ceremony. In writing his own *t'nai-im*, Aaron remarked:

> You are signing a document of what the relationship will become. You are signing a document to be married at a future date. This means that the *t'nai-im* essentially represents what we want our relationship to grow into. And we have it as a constant reminder— even though there are times when we fall short of the ideals, we have these words as our goal.

If you write your own conditions, you are going to have to articulate what is most important to your relationship. In doing this, you will be putting yourself in the document in a profound way. As Aaron's grandmother told him, "Whenever you write something, you put a piece of your soul into it."

Included here are two personalized *t'nai-im* documents (of Craig and Lori and of Rachel and Abe) that focus on the conditions shared by the couple.

T'nai-im of Craig and Lori Sumberg

Surrounded by our family and friends as witnesses and in God's presence, we affirm and celebrate our commitment to one another. As we look forward to our life together, we make the following promises:

To love each other deeply and to share emotional and physical intimacy;

To never lose our sense of humor and to create a marriage and a home filled with love, warmth, patience, creativity, joy, and laughter;

To recognize that sharing a life involves compromise and negotiation, and to work out our differences calmly and lovingly;

To express our emotions in nonthreatening ways whenever possible, to respect each other's opinions and to be sensitive to the other's feelings and needs when communicating;

To accept each other's Jewish beliefs and practices as authentic and deeply held and to challenge each other to be open to spiritual, intellectual, and emotional growth;

To observe and celebrate Shabbat and the Jewish holidays and to create a Jewish home together;

To foster love and respect in our children (that we have them with God's help)—for themselves, for us, and for those around them;

To seek a balance between time spent with ourselves and our children and time spent with our extended families, friends, and community;

To actively encourage each other's professional and personal aspirations and to affirm each other's abilities, especially when the other is most vulnerable; and

To always be mindful that, in so many ways, the world is far from perfect and to continue to do what we can to make it a better place.

The wedding will take place with *mazal tov* and God's will between the bride, Lori Florence Laska, and the groom, Craig Lewis Sumberg, on Saturday night, the 19th of Kislev, November 27, 1999, in New York City, New York.

If either one of us should consider breaking our engagement, a three-part process of evaluation should be undertaken, including personal introspection, an honest and open discussion of our concerns, and counseling with a skilled professional.

These promises were made with mutual understanding and due deliberation and publicly acknowledged on the 16th of Sivan 5759, May 31st, 1999, in Larchmont, New York.

Bride: Groom:
Bride's Father: Groom's Father:
Bride's Mother: Groom's Mother:
Witness: Witness:

T'nai-im of Rachel Bodek and Abe Cohen

In the light of God and encircled by our families and friends, we, Rachel Bodek, *Hebrew Name*, and Abraham Cohen, *Hebrew Name*, agree to marry. As we plan our life together, we promise to fulfill the following conditions. . .

To express love deeply, openly, and with passion
To treat each other with romantic surprises
To listen to each other intently
To nurture each other in the ways each prefers
To find balance in how we express anger
To always put each other above job demands and to be creative and rebellious in this endeavor
To continually renew our friendship and not simply use the other as a repository for daily complaints
To have, with God's help, more than one and less than five children
To respect our own and each other's families
To study Torah together
To pursue intellectual interests together
To respect each other's religious practices

To seal these *t'nai-im*, gifts were exchanged between bride and groom. The groom presented the bride with a beautiful ring. The bride made a donation in honor of the groom's aunt, Joyce Cohen, *z"l*, to Project Judaica.

The wedding will take place, with God's help, on the first day of the week of *Parashat B'midbar* on the 23rd of Iyar in the year 5759, May 9th, 1999.

A fine is to be paid by either party breaking this agreement in the sum of $5000.

All the foregoing was done with perfect understanding and due deliberation. By means of the traditional symbolic transfer, *kinyan*, the mutual agreement of the bride and groom has been confirmed.

_____[Bride]
_____[Groom]
_____[Witness]
_____[Witness]

Putting an Alternative *T'nai-im* Together

If you choose to try writing some of your own *t'nai-im*, consider using a blend of general and specific conditions. The "Conditions and Promises" sections throughout the book are helpful in providing a basis for the *t'nai-im* document. If you did not do those sections of the book, you may want to do them now. You may or may not choose to put the answers to the exercises directly into your document, but they can still be a basis for the language and content you employ in creating your *t'nai-im*.

Handkerchiefs, Broken Plates, and Penalty Meals: The *T'nai-im* Ceremony

Once the document has been written, the next step is to plan the ceremony itself. The *t'nai-im* ceremony can take place anytime and anywhere. You can use it to announce your engagement to others. Or you can use it as a milestone during the engagement. Some couples who are engaged for a year choose to celebrate a *t'nai-im* ceremony three to six months before the wedding. By doing so, the *t'nai-im* ceremony acts as a bridge to the wedding. Planning two ceremonies in close proximity to each other may seem daunting. But the *t'nai-im* ceremony can be as grand or as intimate as you like. Josh and Leah had a simple potluck dinner for their ceremony. Rachel and Abe made up invitations on their computer and had their ceremony in a friend's living room. Some couples do manage to make two big events—it is entirely a matter of personal taste.

You may also worry that having a ceremony so soon before the wedding will make the wedding anticlimactic. But, according to Josh, "It turned out to be the exact opposite." He felt like the *t'nai-im* ceremony prepared him for the wedding in a way that nothing else could have. He began to anticipate the wedding with a deeper sense of commitment to his partner and with greater excitement about the ritual itself.

The brief *t'nai-im* ceremony consists of four parts: *Kiddush*, the reading and signing of the document, *kinyan*, and the breaking of an earthenware dish by the mothers of the couple. These are followed by a meal. If you are having a *t'nai-im* ceremony on a Saturday night, you may want to include *Havdalah* blessings, which are found in appendix 1. So that you can become familiar with each of these elements and decide for yourselves about whether to include them in your celebration, information is provided here about traditional and nontraditional ceremonies.

Kiddush

Judaism transforms ordinary moments into sacred occasions. The most common way to do this is to bless a recognized symbol of joy, a cup of wine:

$$\text{בָּרוּךְ אַתָּה יְיָ אֱלֹהֵינוּ מֶלֶךְ הָעוֹלָם,}$$
$$\text{בּוֹרֵא פְּרִי הַגָּפֶן.}$$

Baruch atah Adonai, Eloheinu Melech haolam, borei p'ri hagafen.

Blessed are You *Adonai*, our God, Ruler of the universe, who creates fruit of the vine.

On joyous occasions, at the beginning of holidays, at the time of first experiencing something, Jews have a custom of saying a prayer of thanks called the *Shehecheyanu:*

$$\text{בָּרוּךְ אַתָּה יְיָ אֱלֹהֵינוּ מֶלֶךְ הָעוֹלָם,}$$
$$\text{שֶׁהֶחֱיָנוּ וְקִיְּמָנוּ וְהִגִּיעָנוּ לַזְּמַן הַזֶּה.}$$

Baruch atah Adonai, Eloheinu Melech haolam, shehecheyanu v'kiy'-manu v'higianu lazman hazeh.

Blessed are You *Adonai*, our God, Ruler of the universe, for giving us life, for sustaining us, and for enabling us to reach this [joyous] moment.

You may also want to write a brief prayer of your own to sanctify the moment. Consider what obstacles you have overcome to get to this moment. Consider other people in your lives who have made this moment possible through their love and support.

Reading and Signing the T'nai-im *Document*

You should decide who will read the *t'nai-im* and in what language it will be written and read. If you choose representatives, perhaps they will read it. If you have someone (a rabbi, cantor, friend, or family member) functioning as your *m'sadeir/m'saderet mitzvah*, the one who arranges your ceremony, this could be part of that person's function as the one who explains and choreographs the proceedings. If you are going to exchange gifts, you can do so as the relevant words of the *t'nai-im* document are read.

Kinyan

For details of the *kinyan*, see page 152. *Kinyan* traditionally follows the reading and signing of the document. If you follow the form of symbolic *kinyan*, you may choose someone you wish to honor to hold the handkerchief and offer it to you.

Breaking of the Dish

In some European Jewish communities, a custom developed of ending the *t'nai-im* ceremony by breaking an earthenware dish, much like weddings end by breaking a glass. In recent years, some liberal couples have chosen to readopt or adapt this custom.

Generally, a pottery dish is used. The mothers of the bride and groom either throw the dish against the floor or a wall, or they hammer the dish to pieces. You can decide what dish to use. Some couples want to use a dish with sentimental value. Others buy a dish specifically for the occasion.

As with many Jewish customs whose original meaning is now unclear, rabbis have offered many explanations for why a dish is broken during the ceremony. Like the breaking of the glass at a wedding, some say we break the dish to remind ourselves of the destruction of the Temple, so that even at this time of joy, we remember the sadness that befell the Jewish people. Others explain we make a sudden crashing noise at joyous times to ward off evil spirits, lest the spirits harm the couple. A medieval commentator warns that engagement is like pottery. Once pottery is broken, it can never be repaired. Therefore, those who enter a *t'nai-im* agreement should never break off the engagement.

Finally, the mothers' breaking a dish is a potent symbol of the changing family bonds between parent and child. The breaking of the dish is meant to symbolize a transformation of the tight bonds between parents and children. For the mothers, breaking the dish acknowledges a new level of separation and their child's new stage of life. For the children, the breaking of the dish releases them to establish enduring emotional bonds with others.

Some couples have interpreted the breaking of the plate differently. They prefer to break the dish themselves, to demonstrate that they are entering into an unbreakable agreement. This, too, is filled with psychological symbolism.

In some communities it is customary for the shards of the dish to be handed to those who are unmarried to express the hope that they, too, will soon experience marriage.

The Knas Mahl—*The Penalty Meal*

Because no Jewish celebration is complete without food, traditionally the ceremony is accompanied by a meal for the guests. Among Jews of Eastern European origin, the special meal following a *t'nai-im* ceremony is known as a *knas mahl*, "penalty meal," to remind everyone of the penalties to be paid if the engagement is broken. Talk about tempering joy with reality! Some communities adopted a custom of eating dairy foods, drawing on a tradition of eating only dairy at Shavuot, the holiday celebrating the marriage of God and Israel through the giving of the Torah. What you choose to eat is entirely up to you.

Tie-Dyes, Vorts, *Sesame Cookies, and White Flowers: Other Events for the Ceremony*

Some couples have used the gathering of friends and relatives at their *t'nai-im* ceremony as a way of preparing for their wedding day. For example, Josh and Leah had all their guests tie-dye square pieces of cloth, which were eventually sewn together to become the *chuppah*, the canopy, at the wedding. Daniel and Tamara had friends write notes to them, which they opened on the early morning of their wedding. The notes were a mixture of blessings and wisdom, meant to prepare and help them on the day of the wedding.

A *vort* of Torah could also be given. A *vort*, Yiddish meaning "a word," colloquially refers to words explaining Torah. At a *t'nai-im* ceremony it refers to a custom in which someone uses words of Torah to speak of the engaged couple's wonderful qualities. Some couples have been honored through the imagery of Mount Sinai, where God married Israel, or through the romantic poetry of Song of Songs. The imagery from the biblical meetings of couples at the well would also be appropriate for a *vort*. You can use any imagery that speaks to you and your guests.

A wide variety of Jewish folk customs arose around engagement. In some parts of Central Europe and Russia, the rabbi drew a circle around the bride and the groom with chalk and inscribed the words *Mazal Tov* in it. The circle is a universally recognized symbol of completion and protection, two characteristics that the couple hoped to find in their relationship. Circle imagery pervades traditional Jewish wedding rituals as well—perfectly round wedding rings and the circling of the bride around the groom (today, often bride and groom circling each other) underneath the *chuppah*.

You may want to consider some more exotic ideas for your *t'nai-im* ceremony. The *t'nai-im* ceremony existed throughout the Jewish world, so there are customs that come from diverse places. The Jews of Cochin

India, for example, had a ceremony whereby all the Jews of the community came together and the eldest member of the community asked the groom whether the match his parents made for him was his desire. He replied, "The desire of my parents is my desire." The elder then posed the same question to the bride, and when the bride also agreed, he blessed a cup of wine and toasted them. The women of the community baked sesame cookies, as a symbol of fertility, and the entire evening was known as sesame evening *(til manda)*. The groom's parents then presented the bride with a small ivory casket filled with jewels.

In the Syrian Jewish community, they did not actually write out a *t'nai-im* document, but they celebrated a party known as "the coming over" to announce an engagement. The party was the last stage in a process. It only occurred after a man had dated a woman a number of times. When he had declared the seriousness of his intentions, his parents met his prospective bride's parents. Privately, they worked out the details of the dowry and the date of the wedding. Then, the prospective groom's parents called the bride's parents to indicate that they would be "coming over," hence the name of the party. Officially, the party was known as *kinyan*. On the day before the "coming over" party, all the guests sent bouquets of flowers in honor of the occasion. There the *shadchan*, the matchmaker responsible for making the match, was treated as a guest of honor. Perhaps if there was someone who acted as your *shadchan*, you can find a way of honoring him or her at your *t'nai-im* celebration.

There's No Sense Crying Over Spilled Wine

With all the pressure of the moment upon him, it was not totally surprising that Josh would knock something over. Josh and Leah had a glass of wine on the table that they had used to make *Kiddush*. After they signed their *t'nai-im* document, Josh knocked over the wine and spilled it right on the *t'nai-im* document, the document that symbolized their first step toward marriage. After cleaning up the spill, they assessed the damage. There was a huge purple splotch on the white space above the words on the *t'nai-im* document and another huge purple splotch on the white space below the words. Their document was not ruined, but neither was it too neat. Some might have taken the spill as a bad omen. But for Josh and Leah what was amazing was that the wine seemed to skip right over the words, making its splotches above and below. The words, which spelled out their commitment to each other and to their shared future, remained untouched.

As you consider marking and celebrating your engagement, you have many options to consider. Its meaning is one that you can choose to share only with each other or with many others. The rich and diverse ways Jews have recognized the power of entering this transitional period, for you and for your family and friends, can help you create your own meaningful *t'nai-im* celebration.

10

On the Threshold of Marriage:
Spiritual Preparation Prior to Your Wedding

> Blessed is the one that comes in the name of God.
>
> Traditional Jewish wedding service

With your ceremony, your relationship to each other will be forever changed. You may want to consider ways to spiritually prepare
yourselves for this life-altering experience as you approach your wedding day. Over the millennia, Jews of different times and cultures have
felt this same need and have created rituals for this purpose. Jews today
are still creating new ways to both highlight and deepen the profoundly
moving and transformative period that precedes a wedding. In the following pages, you will be introduced to some of these customs.

Mikveh

As the sun rose, Randy stood naked on the banks of the Potomac River.
The ten friends with him were fully clothed, watching as he prepared
to enter the water. Though they had been talking and laughing as they
had walked from their cars to the river, they were now silent. The air
was filled with a mixture of excitement and seriousness. With his
friends as witnesses, he was about to carry out the long-standing Jewish
tradition of cleansing himself in running water prior to his wedding. He
and Joan were getting married the next day. As Randy ventured into the
water, he said the words of an ancient blessing, took a deep breath, and

proceeded to dunk his entire body, head to foot, three times. As he came back to the shore, he raced to get his clothes back on before the early-morning kayakers got an unexpected surprise.

The custom of immersing in running water is one that has been practiced for centuries in Jewish communities around the world. In Judaism, as in many other cultures, water is recognized as a medium that facilitates transformation: from womb to independent life; from one religious identity to another; from slave to free person (as in the crossing of the Red Sea); and, as in your case, from single person to married person. Prior to a wedding, it is traditional for both women and men to immerse with the intention of achieving a state of spiritual purity as they begin their new lives together. Immersion can take place in any body of flowing water. The most common choices are rivers and streams or specially designed indoor ritual pools, known as *mikveh*s, which have their own source of untreated rainwater and a system through which water is constantly flowing. In most larger Jewish communities in the United States there is at least one *mikveh*. If this is something you are considering, speak with the rabbi or cantor who will be officiating and discuss your options with them. *Mikveh*s vary in size and elegance. Also, depending upon whose auspices they are under (liberal or Orthodox) there may be conditions or expectations regarding your use of the *mikveh*. Most *mikveh*s require appointments and charge a fee. However, rest assured—despite whatever stories you may have heard from older generations, today's *mikveh*s are clean and welcoming, even sometimes quite beautiful.

Curiously, this seemingly very personal moment is one that, according to tradition, must take place in community. A minyan, a quorum of at least ten, traditionally accompanied bride and groom to an immersion. They served as witnesses, to testify that each member of the couple had followed the prescribed customs and that the wedding would be kosher.

If you choose to include *mikveh* in your pre-wedding plans, you have a number of decisions to make. First, you can decide how closely you wish to adhere to tradition. Second, you can decide if you want to create a community of friends and/or family with whom you share more than your moment of immersion, or if you prefer to do this alone. In recent years, some women have chosen to gather for an evening to share poetry, advice, wisdom, and song, in addition to being present for the immersion in the *mikveh* itself. Third, you can decide which of the options of flowing water you prefer.

A glimpse into the *mikveh* practices of Jews in different parts of the world will help you think creatively about your options. In Syria, the occasion of a bride's going to *mikveh* was celebrated with a party known as *swehni*, an Arabic word meaning "platters." A few nights prior to the wedding, the groom sent the bride a platter with an ornate handbag while she was at her bridal party. Friends also brought gifts, which they placed on the tray. During the party, special sweets and delicacies were eaten. And at the conclusion of the party, the bride went to the *mikveh* accompanied by her female family members and close friends. The bride was traditionally led from her home to the *mikveh* by a group of musicians who sang, danced, and ululated. When the bride got out from the *mikveh*, she was presented with more sweets and coffee. In parts of North Africa, friends on horseback accompanied the groom to a flowing river. There, they sent off a multigun salute for him before he immersed in the water. Following the immersion, they rode back to the home where the wedding would take place, firing their guns as they approached, to alert guests that the wedding was about to take place.

The Procedure

The waters of the *mikveh* must touch every part of the body. Therefore, you must be naked, your hair must be loose, your nails must be clean, and all jewelry and make up must be removed. The goal is to allow the water to envelop you completely, as it did when you were in the womb. Neither your hands nor feet can touch anything, and your eyes should (if possible) remain open.

You immerse yourself once and say:

בָּרוּךְ אַתָּה יְיָ אֱלֹהֵינוּ מֶלֶךְ הָעוֹלָם,
אֲשֶׁר קִדְּשָׁנוּ בְּמִצְוֹתָיו וְצִוָּנוּ עַל הַטְּבִילָה.

Baruch atah Adonai, Eloheinu Melech haolam, asher kid'shanu, b'mitzvotav v'tzivanu al hat'vilah.

Blessed are You *Adonai*, our God, Ruler of the universe, who sanctifies us through the commandments and commands us about immersion.

Immerse yourself one or two more times and then say:

בָּרוּךְ אַתָּה יְיָ אֱלֹהֵינוּ מֶלֶךְ הָעוֹלָם,
שֶׁהֶחֱיָנוּ וְקִיְּמָנוּ וְהִגִּיעָנוּ לַזְּמַן הַזֶּה.

Baruch atah Adonai, Eloheinu Melech haolam, shehecheyanu v'kiy'-manu v'higianu lazman hazeh.

Blessed are You *Adonai*, our God, Ruler of the universe, for giving us life, for sustaining us, and enabling us to reach this [joyous] moment.

Henna

Jews of the Middle East, Far East, and Africa have traditionally prepared the bride and groom for their wedding by applying henna, a brownish-red dye, to various parts of their bodies: hair, hands, feet, arms. In the days immediately prior to the wedding, men gather and help apply henna to the groom, and women gather and help apply henna to the bride. Often it is the same group who go to the *mikveh* who subsequently apply the henna. The henna serves two interrelated purposes. First, it is believed to have a protective effect. The members of a couple, from the time of their engagement until the time of their wedding, are believed to be in a heightened state of vulnerability, which increases as they move nearer to their wedding day. The henna is used to ward off the "evil eye" by altering the natural beauty of the bride or groom, without marring it. Henna is also an adornment, which serves to add beauty to the *mitzvah* of marriage, known in Hebrew as *hidur mitzvah*.

Few western Jews have adopted this particular custom. However, consider what you might do with friends or family to afford yourselves an opportunity to acknowledge your fears and sense of vulnerability, and to provide them an opportunity to offer you their heartfelt wishes for good luck and security.

Simchah and *S'lichah*

Simchah is the Hebrew word for "happiness" or "joy." Jewish weddings and engagements are considered moments of intense joy, cause for great rejoicing. In fact, in the last of the traditional seven blessings offered at a Jewish wedding, the *Sheva B'rachot*, the idea of *simchah* is central: "Soon may there be heard in the streets of Jerusalem, the voice of joy and the voice of happiness [*simchah*], the voice of the groom and the voice of the bride."

S'lichah is the Hebrew word for "contrition" or "forgiveness." You may recognize this word from the prayers said at Yom Kippur. When Jews gather on Yom Kippur, the Day of Atonement, we ask God to forgive us for our various sins: "For all these [sins], God of forgiveness, forgive [*s'lach*] us, pardon us, grant us atonement." On Yom Kippur, we have a chance, at least metaphorically, to start our lives over again, with a clean slate, ready to face the New Year with an openness to unknown possibilities and joy.

As is highlighted by the ritual of going to the *mikveh*, Judaism perceives a link between our ability to truly experience joy and our ability to cleanse our spirits. Seemingly, the cleaner the spirit or soul, the purer the experience of joy. And so, traditionally, prior to a wedding, every effort was made to seek forgiveness, from the living, from the dead, from oneself, and from God.

Judaism teaches that the days leading up to your wedding day are similar to the days leading up to Yom Kippur. These days give you an opportunity to look to the future with joy and to repent for your past, so that you can move forward truly ready for your new life.

Just as on Yom Kippur, when we stand in humility and ask forgiveness from those we have wronged and from God, so too before a wedding it is customary to ask for *s'lichah*, forgiveness, for past wrongs. One traditionally says a *Vidui*, a confessional, on the day of the wedding to accomplish this, the same confessional recited on Yom Kippur. On Yom Kippur, Jews recite the following words as they confess their sins. Some choose to beat their hearts with the confession of each sin; others choose not to. The prayer is written in the plural, "we," because on Yom Kippur we remember our collective and individual guilt.

> For the sin we have committed against You under duress or by choice
> For the sin we have committed against You consciously or unconsciously
> For the sin we have committed against You openly or secretly
> For the sin we have committed against You in our thoughts
> For the sin we have committed against You with our words
> For the sin we have committed against You by the abuse of power
> For all these sins, O God of mercy, forgive us, pardon us, grant us atonement.
> For the sin we have committed against You by hardening our hearts
> For the sin we have committed against You by profaning your name
> For the sin we have committed against You by disrespect for parents and teachers
> For the sin we have committed against You by speaking slander
> For the sin we have committed against You by dishonesty in our work
> For the sin we have committed against You by hurting others in any way
> For all these sins, O God of mercy, forgive us, pardon us, grant us atonement.
>
> *Gates of Atonement,* CCAR

This is, of course, a general confessional. It speaks in the plural, "For the sin *we* have committed." Because it is you alone saying this confessional, consider saying these words in the singular, replacing the "we" with " I," or adding a personal confessional to the general ones. The confessional can be done alone or with a friend, rabbi, or spiritual mentor on the morning of the wedding. Try to do it before you are overwhelmed by other activities.

Judaism teaches that each of us possesses the enduring potential to improve ourselves and our lives. *T'shuvah,* "repenting," literally "rethinking" or "returning"—turning back to God or to ourselves as we know we can be—is, therefore, the single most important act in living a Jewish life. It is the key to our growth and to maintaining a relationship with our own souls, with the people in our lives, and with God.

Personal confession is the first step in the process. The next step is to go to your friends and family and ask them for forgiveness. And, if you and your partner will find it meaningful, do *t'shuvah* with each other. Finally, guarding yourself against repeating the same mistakes in the future is the last step in your personal process. Taking time to think about the situations or temptations that have led you to speak out or act in ways that you later regretted can be a first and necessary step for safeguarding yourselves against repeating the same mistakes in the future.

Memorial Prayers and Visiting Gravesites

> Isaac then brought [Rebekah] into the tent of his mother Sarah, and he took Rebekah as his wife. Isaac loved her and thus found comfort after his mother's death.
>
> Genesis 24:67

When we find a person to love, we often remember others whom we have loved and who have loved us. We often feel a heightened sense of sadness and loss precisely at the times of our greatest joy, because those with whom we want to share our joy are not here to share it with us.

Weddings can be both solace for pain and a reminder of loss. As rabbis we have often heard, "If only my mother/father/grandmother/brother could have lived to see my wedding day." Judaism recognizes our need to acknowledge our sense of loss and longing along with the joy of an upcoming wedding. In some communities, mention is made of deceased relatives and the impact of their absence as part of the ceremony. In others, candles are lit before or during the ceremony, representing a symbolic presence of deceased family members, while other communities have a custom of reciting a traditional Jewish memorial prayer, the *El Malei Rachamim*, at a wedding.

In addition, many Jewish communities have a custom of visiting graves of loved ones, particularly parents, immediately prior to a wedding. Some people find it a comfortable way to gain a sense that a deceased relative is "introduced to" a future spouse and that a deceased parent has the chance to approve of the upcoming wedding.

If you decide to go to the cemetery, what you do at the cemetery is up to you. It should be a time that meets your needs and expectations.

Traditionally, Jews say prayers when they visit a grave. Should you decide to recite prayers, you can find the words to those commonly said at a graveside below. Traditionally, Jews do not visit cemeteries (and, in fact, many Jewish cemeteries are not open) on Jewish holidays, including Shabbat and the week-long holidays of Passover and Sukkot, so plan accordingly.

Psalm 23

מִזְמוֹר לְדָוִד יְהוָה רֹעִי לֹא אֶחְסָר: בִּנְאוֹת דֶּשֶׁא
יַרְבִּיצֵנִי עַל־מֵי מְנֻחוֹת יְנַהֲלֵנִי: נַפְשִׁי יְשׁוֹבֵב יַנְחֵנִי
בְמַעְגְּלֵי־צֶדֶק לְמַעַן שְׁמוֹ: גַּם כִּי־אֵלֵךְ בְּגֵיא צַלְמָוֶת
לֹא־אִירָא רָע כִּי־אַתָּה עִמָּדִי שִׁבְטְךָ וּמִשְׁעַנְתֶּךָ הֵמָּה
יְנַחֲמֻנִי: תַּעֲרֹךְ לְפָנַי שֻׁלְחָן נֶגֶד צֹרְרָי דִּשַּׁנְתָּ בַשֶּׁמֶן
רֹאשִׁי כּוֹסִי רְוָיָה: אַךְ טוֹב וָחֶסֶד יִרְדְּפוּנִי כָּל־יְמֵי חַיָּי
וְשַׁבְתִּי בְּבֵית־יְהוָה לְאֹרֶךְ יָמִים:

Adonai is my shepherd, I shall not want. God makes me lie down in green pastures. God leads me beside still waters. God restores my soul. You lead me in right paths for the sake of Your name. Even when I walk in the valley of the shadow of death, I shall fear no evil, for You are with me, Your rod and staff comfort me. You have set a table before me in the presence of my enemies. You have anointed my head with oil, my cup overflows. Surely goodness and mercy shall follow me all the days of my life, and I shall dwell in the house of *Adonai* forever.

Psalm 130

שִׁיר הַמַּעֲלוֹת מִמַּעֲמַקִּים קְרָאתִיךָ יְהוָה: אֲדֹנָי שִׁמְעָה
בְקוֹלִי תִּהְיֶינָה אָזְנֶיךָ קַשֻּׁבוֹת לְקוֹל תַּחֲנוּנָי:

אִם־עֲוֹנוֹת תִּשְׁמָר־יָהּ אֲדֹנָי מִי יַעֲמֹד: כִּי־עִמְּךָ
הַסְּלִיחָה לְמַעַן תִּוָּרֵא: קִוִּיתִי יְהֹוָה קִוְּתָה נַפְשִׁי
וְלִדְבָרוֹ הוֹחָלְתִּי: נַפְשִׁי לַאדֹנָי מִשֹּׁמְרִים לַבֹּקֶר
שֹׁמְרִים לַבֹּקֶר: יַחֵל יִשְׂרָאֵל אֶל־יְהֹוָה כִּי־עִם־יְהֹוָה
הַחֶסֶד וְהַרְבֵּה עִמּוֹ פְדוּת: וְהוּא יִפְדֶּה אֶת־יִשְׂרָאֵל
מִכֹּל עֲוֹנֹתָיו:

Out of the depths I have cried unto You, God. God, hear my
voice: Let Your ears be attentive to the voice of my supplications.
If You, God, should mark iniquities, God, who could stand? But
there is forgiveness with You, that You may be feared. I wait for
Adonai, my soul waits, and in God's word I do hope. My soul waits
for God, more than watchmen wait for the morning; yea, more
than watchmen for the morning. O let Israel hope in *Adonai*; for
with *Adonai* there is loving-kindness, and with God is plentious
deliverance. And God shall deliver Israel from all their iniquities.

אֵל מָלֵא רַחֲמִים שׁוֹכֵן בַּמְּרוֹמִים, הַמְצֵא מְנוּחָה נְכוֹנָה
תַּחַת כַּנְפֵי הַשְּׁכִינָה. עִם קְדוֹשִׁים וּטְהוֹרִים כְּזוֹהַר הָרָקִיעַ
מַזְהִירִים, אֶת נִשְׁמַת

Say Hebrew name of deceased

Continue here for a man

שֶׁהָלַךְ לְעוֹלָמוֹ. בַּעַל הָרַחֲמִים יַסְתִּירֵהוּ בְּסֵתֶר כְּנָפָיו
לְעוֹלָמִים, וְיִצְרוֹר בִּצְרוֹר הַחַיִּים אֶת נִשְׁמָתוֹ. יְיָ הוּא
נַחֲלָתוֹ. וְיָנוּחַ בְּשָׁלוֹם עַל מִשְׁכָּבוֹ: אָמֵן.

Continue here for a woman

שֶׁהָלְכָה לְעוֹלָמָהּ. בַּעַל הָרַחֲמִים יַסְתִּירֶהָ בְּסֵתֶר כְּנָפָיו
לְעוֹלָמִים, וְיִצְרוֹר בִּצְרוֹר הַחַיִּים אֶת נִשְׁמָתָהּ. יְיָ הוּא
נַחֲלָתָהּ. וְתָנוּחַ בְּשָׁלוֹם עַל מִשְׁכָּבָהּ: אָמֵן.

O God full of compassion, Eternal Spirit of the universe, grant perfect rest under the wings of Your Presence to our loved one who
has entered eternity _____ [loved one's name].
Master of Mercy, let him/her find refuge forever in the shadow of
Your wings, and let his/her soul be bound up in the bond of eternal life. The Eternal God is his/her inheritance. May he/she rest in
peace. Amen.

Fasting

While most liberal Jews associate fasting only with Yom Kippur, there
are various times on the annual Jewish calendar and during a Jew's lifetime that the tradition prescribes a fast. The wedding day is one such
time. Again, as a way of recognizing and highlighting your emotional
and spiritual preparation for this major transition, Jewish tradition prescribes a physical component as well. This fast, as with the Yom Kippur
fast, is intended to draw your focus away from the material world to the
spiritual world. The fast can be a means for you to reflect on your life
and to seek forgiveness from God and yourself, so that you can move
into the next stage of your life with an overwhelming sense of joy and
hope, of ever expanding possibilities for growth and change. Your transition from *s'lichah* to *simchah* is officially over when you drink wine as
part of your ceremony, thus breaking your fast and celebrating the joy
and holiness of the moment. Traditionally, you eat your first meal of the
day as a married person, shared with your new spouse.

Fasts, of course, are not for everyone. If you get queasy or
light-headed from fasting, it's probably not an option to consider on

your wedding day. You might also consider some sort of modified fast, particularly if you are planning for an evening wedding. If fasting is a spiritual discipline that appeals to you, you might consider it for a different day in close proximity to your wedding.

11

Chanukat HaBayit: Dedicating Your Home

May this home be blessed with much joy.
May this home be blessed with many little ones.
May this home be a refuge for both of you.
May this home be a shared space of growth and wisdom.
May this home always have a well-stocked refrigerator.

These words are some among many that Jews have said as they have dedicated a home. Judaism recognizes that a home is more than just a structure. It is a space that can be a source of holiness and meaning. To affirm this belief, Jews customarily celebrate moving into a new home with a ceremony known in Hebrew as *chanukat habayit,* "dedication of the home." The ceremony is usually celebrated at the time of or soon after an individual, couple, or family moves into a new home.

You may recognize the first word of the name, *chanukat,* because of its similarity to the name of the Jewish holiday of Chanukah. The eight-day holiday, best known for the lighting of candles, the eating of potato pancakes (latkes), and the miracle of the oil, commemorates the rededication of the Second Temple, the Israelites' House of Prayer, after it had been desecrated. According to the story, King Antiochus, leader of the Assyrian-Greeks, ordered his troops to bring idols and pigs into the Second Temple. When the Maccabees recaptured the Temple, they needed to clean it and reconsecrate it for religious rituals.

Jews have chosen to mark the moment of establishing a new home through a dedication ceremony as well. The Jewish home has been called a *mikdash m'at,* "a small sanctuary." Your sanctuary, your home, can also be a place where holiness is affirmed and present.

How can you affirm holiness in your home?

Rabbi Yosei ben Yochanan says, "Let your house be wide open, and let the poor be members of your household."

Pirkei Avot 1:5

In a midrash seen earlier, Rabban Shimon ben Gamliel says:

Those who cause peace to reign in their house are regarded as though they have caused peace between every individual in Israel, and those who cause jealousy and contention to reign in their house are regarded as though they have caused jealousy and contention to reign in all of Israel.

Avot D'Rabbi Natan 28:3

Establishing your home together is an appropriate time to find ways to follow the words of Rabbi Yosei, creating a space that reflects both your openness to community and your commitment to charity. As you have worked through the chapters of this book, hopefully you have gained insights into the ways the two of you can create and maintain peace in your home, *sh'lom bayit*. Judaism teaches that a home that reflects a commitment to peace, community, and charity becomes a gateway to holiness for all who enter it.

The simple *chanukat habayit* ceremony affirms these commitments. Even if you are already living together, there are ways for you to symbolically and ritually affirm the type of home you want to establish.

The ritual of *chanukat habayit* has two major elements: a mezuzah is affixed to a doorway, and blessings are said. If you have already been living together and have put up a mezuzah on the front doorway, but did not have a *chanukat habayit* ceremony, it is not too late. Consider having the ceremony as you put up a mezuzah on the door of one of the other principal rooms of your home. If you have been living together for a while, the ceremony can be used as a way to highlight and celebrate your changed status.

The Mezuzah

The mezuzah is one of the primary symbols of the Jewish home. The Hebrew word *mezuzah* literally means "doorpost." In the Torah, in Deuteronomy 6:9, God tells the people of Israel, "And [you will] inscribe them [these words of God] on the doorposts of your house and upon your gates." Clearly, all of God's words could not be placed on the doorposts and gates of a house. So the custom developed of writing the passage containing the commandment regarding doorposts onto a small piece of parchment that, covered, could be easily affixed to a doorpost. In this way, as a Jew came or went from home, the symbol could be a reminder of an enduring relationship with God and of the need to reflect that relationship in deeds carried out both inside and outside the home. The parchment, in Hebrew a *k'laf*, has passages from Deuteronomy 6:4–9 and 11:13–21 written on one side and the word *Shaddai* (Almighty) on the other side. Mezuzot (plural of "mezuzah") containers come in all shapes, sizes, and materials. Some are clear, so that the word *Shaddai* on the scroll is visible. Others, made of non-translucent materials like wood, ceramic, or silver, have either the word *Shaddai* inscribed on them or just the first letter of the word, a *shin*.

As with so many inherited Jewish customs, there are a multitude of explanations regarding the purpose and function of the mezuzah. For many centuries, particularly in the Middle Ages, many Jews believed the mezuzah was an amulet that protected their house from evil demons and destructive forces. Some claim that the word *Shaddai* can be read as an anagram for the phrase, *Shomeir d'latot Yisrael*, which means "Guardian of the doors of Israel." This common perception was even recognized by rabbinic authorities. Meir of Rothenberg, a prominent medieval rabbinical authority said:

> The Jewish people may be assured that no demon can have power over a house upon which the mezuzah is properly affixed. In our house I believe we have close to twenty-four mezuzot.
>
> Quoted by Joshua Trachtenberg,
> in *Jewish Magic and Superstition*, 1961

This belief was so dominant that at times Jews blamed plagues and disasters that befell their communities upon improperly written, old, or improperly hung mezuzot. To enhance the power of the mezuzah, some Jews even added names of angels or a Star of David to the parchment.

More rationally inclined rabbis and communities denounced and rejected these superstitious folk practices. Maimonides, the most famous of these leaders, wrote:

> Fools pervert for temporal benefit the religious duty of the mezuzah, of proclaiming the Unity of God and the love and service due to God, as though this were an amulet.

He believed the purpose of affixing a mezuzah was clear:

> By the commandment of the mezuzah, man is reminded, when entering or departing [his home], of God's Unity, and is stirred into love for God. This contemplation brings him back to himself and leads him on the right path.
>
> *Yad, T'fillin* 5:4

In response to such vehement opposition, those who believed in the magical powers of the mezuzah tried to subvert condemnation by creating a cryptogram on the back of the mezuzah. The cryptogram substituted each letter of a three-word Hebrew phrase, "God is our God," with the next letter of the alphabet. *Yod* became *kaf, hei* became *vav,* and so on. The new letter sequences were nonsensical to those who did not know how to break the code. Quite remarkably, this cryptogram can still be found on the back of every mezuzah to this day!

The mezuzah is also seen by some as a mark of distinction. Like wearing a *chai* around your neck or a *kippah* on your head, a mezuzah on your door is a public declaration and affirmation of your Jewishness. For many Jews in today's world, hanging a mezuzah on their home or wearing one around their neck serves as an important symbol of Jewish identity.

Whether or not any of these reasons resonates with you, consider how each of the purported functions of the mezuzah can have meaning for you and the home you are establishing. You probably aspire to have a space that offers protection—physical, emotional, and spiritual; a place that helps you connect with, affirm, and develop the various parts of your identity; and finally, a place in which you are constantly reminded of the holy, of God's presence, in your lives. How are you going to consciously reflect these values in your home? Consider how you can incorporate these ideas into the ceremony at the end of this chapter.

Hanging the Mezuzah Diagonally:
A Talmudic Lesson in Compromise

A mezuzah is hung diagonally upon the upper part of the right-hand door lintel. It certainly would be simpler to hang it vertically or horizontally. But according to custom, it must be hung diagonally. As with so many points of Jewish law and custom, the answer can be traced back to a medieval argument regarding a talmudic text. Apparently in the eleventh and twelfth centuries, there was considerable disagreement about the proper way to hang a mezuzah. Rashi (Rabbi Shlomo ben Yitzchak, 1040–1105, who lived in France), perhaps the most well-known and respected biblical and talmudic commentator, argued that it should hang vertically. His reasoning was based on the Sephardic custom of holding the Torah up while it was being read. His grandsons and their generation, raised in an Ashkenazic milieu in which the Torah was customarily read when laid flat, or horizontally, advised that the mezuzah hang horizontally. Ultimately, the custom arose of hanging the mezuzah diagonally, as a compromise between the two positions.

Today, the exact way the compromise was reached is lost. However, the result is interesting. The customs related to the quintessential symbol of a Jewish home are the result of a compromise! And prior to that compromise, there had been no single, agreed upon manner for Jews to correctly fulfill the commandment of hanging a mezuzah. The parallels with your relationship and your home are fairly obvious. Real relationships require compromise. You have come to each other with different perspectives, perceptions, histories, and patterns of behavior, and eventually you will find ways to honor your differences and establish compromises with which you can both comfortably live. Each time you come and go from your home, the mezuzah can be a reminder of the power of compromise.

Even the idea of a diagonal is instructive for relationships. You should not be vertical in your relationship, that is, you should not stand aloof from your partner, unwilling to bend to anything your partner may want. Neither should you be flat, always willing to do whatever your partner wants, even if it is contrary to your own needs and desires. You should approach your partner diagonally, aware of what you need, yet always inclining toward your partner to see what your partner needs, ready and willing to compromise.

The *Chanukat HaBayit* Ceremony

The *chanukat habayit* ceremony is typically an informal gathering of friends and family. The presence of a rabbi or cantor is not necessary. But if you have a relationship with such a person, or if having a clergy person present will enhance the meaning of the moment for you, you may consider consulting with or inviting a rabbi or cantor to facilitate the ritual.

As with most Jewish ceremonies, the *chanukat habayit* is traditionally followed by a festive meal. Through the sharing of food, you and your guests can be reminded of the fullness and festivity that you hope will be a part of your home. The most commonly cited textual base for this practice comes from *Midrash Tanchuma:*

> The Holy One blessed and sanctified the Shabbat upon completing the world, like a human being who builds a house and then makes a feast.

Just as at a wedding, where a glass is broken to remember the destruction of Jerusalem, so too in completing a home is there a remembrance of that destruction:

> In the Tosefta, it says: A person whitewashes their house with lime, and leaves a little portion [of their wall] unfinished in remembrance of the destruction of Jerusalem.
>
> *Tosefta, Bava Batra* 2:17

The destruction of Jerusalem has come to be Judaism's symbolic means of referring to a world that is somehow incomplete, a still-broken world in which pain is present, a world that we, as Jews, are responsible to help repair. Our task is to contribute to *tikkun olam*—mending the world. A unique part of the *chanukat habayit* ceremony in this book is its recommendation that you "unfinish" something.

In some communities, Jews leave a symbolic part of their home unfinished during construction. Though you are unlikely to actually build your own home, you will probably oversee the painting or repairs. You can leave a small spot on a lintel, or on a closet ceiling, unpainted and thus unfinished. Then, during your ceremony and in days thereafter, you can take note of the spot and be reminded of your sacred responsibility to help repair the world.

There are also a variety of other Jewish customs from around the world for dedicating a home. You may want to use some of them creatively in the ceremony. Some of these customs originated in distant Jewish communities, places that may feel far removed from your Jewish life. However, Jewish customs from these diverse places are part of the rich tapestry of Jewish life, and they are part of your cultural and spiritual heritage.

These customs symbolizing sweetness, abundance, fertility, and happiness were normally celebrated after the marriage, when the bride was entering her future home.

In arid Libya, the groom traditionally dropped an earthenware pitcher of water from the roof of the home he and his bride would inhabit. After it fell, the bride walked through the broken pottery and the water. In some of Jerusalem's Sephardic communities, a specially baked cake, called *ruksah*, was broken over the heads of the bride and groom. In Baghdad, a similiar custom existed, but it was carried out with loaves of bread. In Turkey, it was customary for a sheep to be slaughtered as a sacrifice. The meat was given away to the poor, not eaten by the couple or their guests. A provision was made for those too poor to afford a sheep; fowl could be slaughtered instead. In Georgia, Russia, the doorposts of the couple's home were smeared with butter and honey, reminders of the biblical symbols of the abundance of the Promised Land, milk and honey. And finally, in Salonika, Greece, the groom stood at the top of the stairs and threw rice and coins at the feet of his bride. In many parts of Eastern Europe, guests brought bread, wine, and salt—so that the inhabitants of the house would always have life's necessities and joy.

Besides creatively using some of the customs above or letting them inspire you to create your own ritual actions, you may want to include songs or *divrei Torah* (words of Torah) in the ceremony. The entire ceremony usually lasts but a few minutes. Today, some couples use it as a time to share their dreams and associations for the home they are establishing. The structure of the ceremony is very basic. The one included here can be used as is or adapted in whatever ways are comfortable and meaningful for you.

Chanukat HaBayit Ceremony

The ceremony begins with your friends and family gathered directly outside your door.

The following is said:

> As the mezuzah is a symbol of Jewish identity, we dedicate this home to preserving and treasuring our Jewish identity.
>
> As the mezuzah is an amulet of protection, so we dedicate this home to protecting each other as best as we can from isolation, fear, pain, and loneliness.
>
> As the mezuzah reminds us daily of God's presence, so we dedicate this home to acting in the way of the Divine.

> We dedicate this home also to: [consider other values you want to see reflected in your home].

Read or chant Deuteronomy 6:4–9:

שְׁמַ֖ע יִשְׂרָאֵ֑ל יְהֹוָ֥ה אֱלֹהֵ֖ינוּ יְהֹוָ֥ה אֶחָֽד׃ וְאָֽהַבְתָּ֖ אֵ֚ת
יְהֹוָ֣ה אֱלֹהֶ֑יךָ בְּכָל־לְבָֽבְךָ֖ וּבְכָל־נַפְשְׁךָ֖ וּבְכָל־מְאֹדֶֽךָ׃
וְהָי֞וּ הַדְּבָרִ֣ים הָאֵ֗לֶּה אֲשֶׁ֨ר אָֽנֹכִ֧י מְצַוְּךָ֖ הַיּ֑וֹם
עַל־לְבָבֶֽךָ׃ וְשִׁנַּנְתָּ֣ם לְבָנֶ֔יךָ וְדִבַּרְתָּ֖ בָּ֑ם בְּשִׁבְתְּךָ֣
בְּבֵיתֶ֗ךָ וּבְלֶכְתְּךָ֤ בַדֶּ֨רֶךְ֙ וּֽבְשָׁכְבְּךָ֖ וּבְקוּמֶֽךָ׃ וּקְשַׁרְתָּ֥ם
לְא֖וֹת עַל־יָדֶ֑ךָ וְהָי֥וּ לְטֹטָפֹ֖ת בֵּ֥ין עֵינֶֽיךָ׃ וּכְתַבְתָּ֛ם
עַל־מְזֻז֥וֹת בֵּיתֶ֖ךָ וּבִשְׁעָרֶֽיךָ׃

Hear, O Israel! *Adonai* is our God, *Adonai* is One. You shall love *Adonai* your God with all of your heart, with all of your soul, and with all of your might. Take to heart these instructions with which I charge you this day. Teach them to your children. Recite them when you stay at home and when you are away, when you lie down and when you rise up. Bind them as a sign upon your hand. Let them serve as a symbol on your forehead. Inscribe them on the doorposts of your house, and upon your gates.

Holding the mezuzah, say the following:

בָּרוּךְ אַתָּה יְיָ אֱלֹהֵינוּ מֶלֶךְ הָעוֹלָם,
אֲשֶׁר קִדְּשָׁנוּ בְּמִצְוֹתָיו וְצִוָּנוּ לִקְבּוֹעַ מְזוּזָה.

Baruch atah Adonai, Eloheinu Melech haolam, asher kid'shanu b'mitzvotav v'tzivanu likboa mezuzah.

Blessed are You *Adonai*, our God, Ruler of the universe, who sanctifies us through the commandments and commands us to affix the mezuzah.

Affix the mezuzah to the right doorpost as one enters the home, with the top part inclined toward the inside of the home. The mezuzah should be affixed at the upper part of the doorpost (about eye level for a six-foot person).

After the mezuzah is affixed, say the following:

בָּרוּךְ אַתָּה יְיָ אֱלֹהֵינוּ מֶלֶךְ הָעוֹלָם,
שֶׁהֶחֱיָנוּ וְקִיְּמָנוּ וְהִגִּיעָנוּ לַזְּמַן הַזֶּה.

Baruch atah Adonai, Eloheinu Melech haolam, shehecheyanu v'kiy'-manu v'higianu lazman hazeh.

Blessed are you *Adonai*, our God, Ruler of the universe, for giving us life, for sustaining us, and for enabling us to reach this [joyous] moment.

Ask for blessings upon the new home from everyone gathered.

Read or chant Deuteronomy 11:13–21:

וְהָיָ֗ה אִם־שָׁמֹ֤עַ תִּשְׁמְעוּ֙ אֶל־מִצְוֺתַ֔י אֲשֶׁ֧ר אָנֹכִ֛י מְצַוֶּ֥ה
אֶתְכֶ֖ם הַיּ֑וֹם לְאַהֲבָ֞ה אֶת־יְהֹוָ֤ה אֱלֹֽהֵיכֶם֙ וּלְעָבְד֔וֹ
בְּכׇל־לְבַבְכֶ֖ם וּבְכׇל־נַפְשְׁכֶֽם: וְנָתַתִּ֧י מְטַֽר־אַרְצְכֶ֛ם
בְּעִתּ֖וֹ יוֹרֶ֣ה וּמַלְק֑וֹשׁ וְאָסַפְתָּ֣ דְגָנֶ֔ךָ וְתִירֹֽשְׁךָ֖ וְיִצְהָרֶֽךָ:
וְנָתַתִּ֛י עֵ֥שֶׂב בְּשָׂדְךָ֖ לִבְהֶמְתֶּ֑ךָ וְאָכַלְתָּ֖ וְשָׂבָֽעְתָּ:
הִשָּׁמְר֣וּ לָכֶ֔ם פֶּ֥ן יִפְתֶּ֖ה לְבַבְכֶ֑ם וְסַרְתֶּ֗ם וַעֲבַדְתֶּם֙
אֱלֹהִ֣ים אֲחֵרִ֔ים וְהִשְׁתַּחֲוִיתֶ֖ם לָהֶֽם: וְחָרָ֨ה אַף־יְהֹוָ֜ה
בָּכֶ֗ם וְעָצַ֤ר אֶת־הַשָּׁמַ֙יִם֙ וְלֹֽא־יִהְיֶ֣ה מָטָ֔ר וְהָ֣אֲדָמָ֔ה לֹ֥א
תִתֵּ֖ן אֶת־יְבוּלָ֑הּ וַאֲבַדְתֶּ֣ם מְהֵרָ֗ה מֵעַל֙ הָאָ֣רֶץ הַטֹּבָ֔ה
אֲשֶׁ֥ר יְהֹוָ֖ה נֹתֵ֣ן לָכֶֽם: וְשַׂמְתֶּ֞ם אֶת־דְּבָרַ֣י אֵ֗לֶּה
עַל־לְבַבְכֶ֖ם וְעַֽל־נַפְשְׁכֶ֑ם וּקְשַׁרְתֶּ֨ם אֹתָ֤ם לְאוֹת֙
עַל־יֶדְכֶ֔ם וְהָי֥וּ לְטוֹטָפֹ֖ת בֵּ֥ין עֵינֵיכֶֽם: וְלִמַּדְתֶּ֥ם אֹתָ֛ם
אֶת־בְּנֵיכֶ֖ם לְדַבֵּ֣ר בָּ֑ם בְּשִׁבְתְּךָ֤ בְּבֵיתֶ֙ךָ֙ וּבְלֶכְתְּךָ֣ בַדֶּ֔רֶךְ
וּֽבְשׇׁכְבְּךָ֖ וּבְקוּמֶֽךָ: וּכְתַבְתָּ֛ם עַל־מְזוּז֥וֹת בֵּיתֶ֖ךָ
וּבִשְׁעָרֶֽיךָ: לְמַ֨עַן יִרְבּ֤וּ יְמֵיכֶם֙ וִימֵ֣י בְנֵיכֶ֔ם עַ֚ל הָֽאֲדָמָ֔ה
אֲשֶׁ֨ר נִשְׁבַּ֧ע יְהֹוָ֛ה לַאֲבֹתֵיכֶ֖ם לָתֵ֣ת לָהֶ֑ם כִּימֵ֥י הַשָּׁמַ֖יִם
עַל־הָאָֽרֶץ:

If, then, you obey the commandments that I enjoin upon you this day, loving the Lord your God, and serving *Adonai* with all your heart and soul, I will grant the rain for your land in season, with early rain and the late. You shall gather in your new grain and wine and oil—I will also provide grass in the fields for your cattle—and thus you shall eat your fill. Take care not to be lured away to serve other gods and bow to them. For the Lord's anger will flare up against you, and *Adonai* will shut up the skies so that there will be no rain and the ground will not yield its produce; and you will soon perish from the good land that the Lord is giving you. Therefore impress these My words upon your very heart: bind them as a sign on your hand and let them serve as a symbol on your forehead, and teach them to your children—reciting them when you stay at home and when you are away, when you lie down and when you rise up, and inscribe them on the doorposts of your house and upon your gates—to the end that you and your children may endure, in the land that the Lord swore to your fathers to give to them, as long as there is a heaven over the earth.

If you have left some part of the home unfinished, point it out and say the following:

> Jewish tradition tells us that in creating a new home, it is customary to leave some small piece of it unfinished. This is to remind us that the world is still unfinished. There are people who do not have homes, who are in need of our help. Let this spot be a reminder to us that our task is to mend the pain in this world.

Read Psalm 121:8:

יְהֹוָה יִשְׁמָר־צֵאתְךָ וּבוֹאֶךָ מֵעַתָּה וְעַד־עוֹלָם:

Adonai yishmar tzeitcha uvo-echa mei-atah v'ad olam.

May God guard you when you go out and when you come in, now and forever!

A Liberal Jewish Perspective on Moving in Together before Marriage

Including a ritual for moving in together in a book about Jewish engagement reflects our presumption that many of you are either already living together or will be before your wedding day. While Judaism has traditionally condemned premarital intimacy, it is also true that Judaism has been relatively liberal in the area of sexuality compared to other religious traditions. Today, moving in together before marriage has become an accepted practice in liberal Jewish circles, as it is in society at large. Rarely will you hear a liberal Jewish leader speak about the dangers of living together. Not all couples choose this option of course, but the stigma of "living in sin," as an earlier generation might have called it, is gone.

For most couples today, the determination of whether to move in together before marriage has less to do with the morality of the matter, and more to do with issues of commitment or economics. Some couples move in together because one or both members of the couple want to test the relationship before committing to marriage. They want to be sure that their partner is right for them, and they feel that the only way to figure that out is to live together before getting married. Other couples specifically do not move in together because they do not want to be in a test. They feel that if they are ready to move in together, then they are ready for marriage.

Can Judaism shed any light on the decision of moving in together before marriage? A liberal Jewish perspective does have something to say about this issue, but it is not a simple yes or no statement.

One of the values central to an intimate relationship is *emet* (truth). Reform rabbis have affirmed that authentic and ethical human relationships should be grounded in both truth and honesty. As you decide about living together before marriage, keep this value in mind. Have you each been truthful with your partner about your understanding of where the relationship is heading? Is moving in together a test? Does moving in together imply a commitment to marry some time in the future? Do you weigh the seriousness of living together in the same way? Inevitably lives become intertwined, and if one member of the couple is approaching the situation without accepting this, problems can arise. Reform Judaism, therefore, counsels that couples move in together only if they are being completely truthful with themselves and each other about their feelings and their expectations. (See appendix 3 for the text of the Central Conference of American Rabbis Ad Hoc Committee on Human Sexuality, Report to the CCAR Convention, June 1998.)

Additional Resources

For further examples of *chanukat habayit* ceremonies, see the following:

Gates of the House. New York: CCAR Press, 1997, 103–107.

Siegel, Richard, Michael Strassfeld, and Sharon Strassfeld, eds. *The First Jewish Catalogue.* Philadelphia: Jewish Publication Society, 1989, 15.

Stern, Chaim, ed. *On the Doorposts of Your House: Prayers and Ceremonies for the Jewish Home.* New York: CCAR Press, 1994, 138–142.

Havdalah (For a Saturday Night *T'nai-im* Ceremony)

Havdalah is the ritual to mark the end of Shabbat. *Havdalah* means "separation," and the ceremony so named separates Shabbat from the rest of the week. If you are having a *t'nai-im* ceremony on a Saturday night, you may want to include a *Havdalah* ceremony, especially since your engagement marks an important separation as well. You are separating from your pasts. Boundaries are changing at this transitional moment. Family allegiances, future expectations, ideas about property are all in flux. You are making a commitment that much of what has been just yours will now become both of yours. The *Havdalah* ceremony can ritualize this transition.

Havdalah can take place at the beginning of the ceremony in place of the *Kiddush*, because it includes a blessing over wine. For the ceremony, you will need a cup of wine, a container of spices, and a special multi-wicked *Havdalah* candle. According to midrash, the *Havdalah* blessings were first uttered by Adam in the Garden of Eden on the very first Shabbat. Banished from the garden, he grew fearful of the coming darkness. God then instructed Adam that in rubbing stones together he could create a spark, which would create flames to give him warmth and light. As he did so, he said a blessing.

Havdalah *Blessings*

THE WINE OR GRAPE JUICE

בָּרוּךְ אַתָּה יְיָ אֱלֹהֵינוּ מֶלֶךְ הָעוֹלָם,
בּוֹרֵא פְּרִי הַגָּפֶן.

Baruch atah Adonai, Eloheinu Melech haolam, borei p'ri hagafen.

Blessed are You, *Adonai* our God, Ruler of the universe, who creates the fruit of the vine.

(The leader does not drink the wine or grape juice until after the final blessing, when *Havdalah* has been completed.)

THE SPICES

בָּרוּךְ אַתָּה יְיָ, אֱלֹהֵינוּ מֶלֶךְ הָעוֹלָם,
בּוֹרֵא מִינֵי בְשָׂמִים:

Baruch atah Adonai, Eloheinu Melech haolam, borei minei v'samim.

Blessed are You, *Adonai* our God, Ruler of the universe, who creates the world's spices.

(The spice box is now circulated.)

THE LIGHT

Raise the *Havdalah* candle.

בָּרוּךְ אַתָּה יְיָ, אֱלֹהֵינוּ מֶלֶךְ הָעוֹלָם,
בּוֹרֵא מְאוֹרֵי הָאֵשׁ:

Baruch atah Adonai, Eloheinu Melech haolam, borei m'orei ha-eish.

Blessed are You, *Adonai* our God, Ruler of the universe, who creates fire.

The candle is held high as the leader says:

בָּרוּךְ אַתָּה יְיָ, אֱלֹהֵינוּ מֶלֶךְ הָעוֹלָם, הַמַּבְדִּיל
בֵּין קֹדֶשׁ לְחוֹל, בֵּין אוֹר לְחֹשֶׁךְ, בֵּין יִשְׂרָאֵל
לָעַמִּים, בֵּין יוֹם הַשְּׁבִיעִי, לְשֵׁשֶׁת יְמֵי הַמַּעֲשֶׂה:
בָּרוּךְ אַתָּה יְיָ, הַמַּבְדִּיל בֵּין קֹדֶשׁ לְחוֹל:

Baruch atah Adonai, Eloheinu Melech haolam, hamavdil bein kodesh l'chol, bein or l'choshech, bein Yisrael laamim, bein yom hash'vi-i l'sheishet y'mei hamaaseh. Baruch atah Adonai, hamavdil bein kodesh l'chol.

We praise You, Eternal God, Sovereign of the universe: You make distinctions, teaching us to distinguish the commonplace from the holy; You create light and darkness, Israel and the nations, the seventh day of rest and the six days of labor.

We praise You, O God: You call us to distinguish the commonplace from the holy.

Sip the wine or grape juice.

Extinguish the *Havdalah* candle in the remaining wine or grape juice, while the following passages are sung or said:

הַמַּבְדִּיל בֵּין–קֹדֶשׁ לְחֹל.
חַטֹּאתֵינוּ הוּא יִמְחֹל.
זַרְעֵנוּ וְכַסְפֵּנוּ יַרְבֶּה כַּחוֹל.
וְכַכּוֹכָבִים בַּלָּיְלָה.

Hamavdil bein kodesh l'chol, chatoteinu hu yimchol, zareinu v'chaspeinu yarbeh kachol, v'chakochavim balailah.

Shavua tov

A good week, a week of peace.
May gladness reign and joy increase.

Eliyahu HaNavi

אֵלִיָּהוּ הַנָּבִיא, אֵלִיָּהוּ הַתִּשְׁבִּי,
אֵלִיָּהוּ, אֵלִיָּהוּ, אֵלִיָּהוּ הַגִּלְעָדִי.
בִּמְהֵרָה בְיָמֵינוּ, יָבוֹא אֵלֵינוּ,
עִם מָשִׁיחַ בֶּן–דָּוִד,
עִם מָשִׁיחַ בֶּן–דָּוִד.
אֵלִיָּהוּ . . .

Eliyahu HaNavi, Eliyahu HaTishbi,
Eliyahu, Eliyahu, Eliyahu HaGiladi.

Bim'heirah v'yameinu, yavo eileinu,
im Mashiach ben David,
im Mashiach ben David.
Eliyahu HaNavi . . .

Elijah the prophet, the Tishbite, the Gileadite: come to us soon, to herald our redemption . . .

Havdalah: *An Exercise in Separation*

Your separation from your pasts is, of course, different from the separation between Shabbat and the workweek. Therefore, you may want to include your own blessing of separation along with the traditional blessings. Consider the significant separations you are experiencing at this point in your life. Perhaps you are moving away from friends or moving out of a home you share with others. Decide if including a blessing of separation for yourself will feel appropriate at your ceremony.

The Origins of the *T'nai-im* Ceremony

The *t'nai-im* ceremony arose after the Middle Ages, but its roots go back to the Talmud, which scholars believe was completed around 600 C.E. According to the Talmud, the families of the bride and groom were responsible for negotiating the terms of the marriage, such as the dowry and gifts to be exchanged between families. These conditions were called the *t'na-ei shiduchin*, which would later serve as the basis for the standard *t'nai-im* document. The Talmud holds that it is crucial that *t'na-ei shiduchin* are worked out before a marriage: *ein m'kad'shin b'li shiduchin*, "there should be no marriage without the agreement" (BT *kiddushin* 12b). The Talmud also says that those who went ahead and married without agreeing to conditions were subject to flogging. Given the importance of making these agreements, the Talmud allows for marriage negotiations to take place even on Shabbat, when it is normally forbidden to discuss business matters.

After the *t'na-ei shiduchin* were agreed to, the formal betrothal ceremony took place. Marriage in the talmudic period actually consisted of two parts separated by a year. The first part, which is the formal act of betrothal, is known as either *eirusin* or *kiddushin*. At this betrothal ceremony, the groom would present the bride with an object of some value, often a ring, in front of witnesses. Accompanying the gift would be an oral or written document (known as a *sh'tar*), which would declare the groom's intention to marry the bride. The betrothal ceremony had a legal status. Although they were still not husband and wife, the woman was not sexually permitted to anybody else. The second part of the wedding, which took place months later, was called *nisuin*, the bringing together of the bride and the groom underneath the *chuppah*. If the bride or the bridegroom wished to dissolve the relationship after completing the first part of the marriage ceremony, but not the second, they would need to have a formal divorce. They would also be subject to a penalty by the rabbinical courts for breaching the promise to complete the marriage, and all gifts exchanged between the families would be returned.

Around the eleventh century, the two parts of the marriage ceremony merged, giving us the wedding ceremony we know today. The wedding ring is given underneath the *chuppah*, and the well-known phrase "you are consecrated to me with this ring, according to the laws of Moses and Israel" and the *Sheva B'rachot*, "Seven Blessings," are recited to consecrate the marriage.

Why the two parts of the wedding were merged is not totally clear. Perhaps it was simply the expense of having two different events, which was difficult for poor families. Perhaps it was easier and safer to bring everyone together just once. Because the two ceremonies merged and there was no longer a separate *kiddushin* (betrothal) ceremony, there was a need to formalize the *t'na-ei shiduchin* (marriage agreement) between families. *T'nai-im* is the name of the document that formalized the arrangements, and the celebration surrounding the signing of the document is known as the *t'nai-im* ceremony.

Reform Jewish Sexual Values

Central Conference of American Rabbis
Ad Hoc Committee on Human Sexuality
Selig Salkowtiz, Chair
Report to the CCAR Convention, June 1998

I. MISSION STATEMENT

As liberal Jews, we seek to understand human sexuality and sexual expression in a religious context. While we are aware that at this point in our history the value systems of many liberal Jews are based upon contemporary secular norms, it is our belief that Reform Judaism can speak meaningfully to all aspects of our lives, including intimate human relationships. In framing a religious value system that can guide all of us in making decisions about our sexuality, we utilize religious principles derived from our Reform predecessors. These principles are based upon the threefold approach which Reform Judaism has developed in the course of its history: universalism, particularism, and contemporary knowledge. This threefold approach can be expressed through the following guiding principles:

(1) *B'riah* (The Created Universe): We exist as part of a vast and varied world fashioned by a purposeful Creator. "When God created humanity, God made Adam in the Divine image . . . male and female . . . and God found it very good" (Genesis 1:27, 31). Creator and creature are bound together through this intentional act. *B'riah* reminds us that our human uniqueness and diversity, including our sexuality, are ultimately derived from the conscious Divine act of creation and as such are purposeful and positive.

(2) *Am B'rit* (People of the Covenant): As Jews we also exist as part of a particular people which has a unique and holy relation-

ship with God. After entering into covenant with God at Sinai, our people responded by saying, "All that the Eternal God has spoken we will faithfully do" (Exodus 24:7). Each generation, like the first one at Sinai, is committed to responsible action, the essential confirmation of belief. We share a special mandate to preserve this relationship through the Jewish generations of history. We weigh the many voices of our tradition as we seek to find ways for modern Jews to express themselves as sexual beings in an authentically Jewish manner.

(3) **Daat** (Contemporary Knowledge): Yosef Albo, a noted medieval Jewish philosopher wrote, "It is impossible that the law of God. . . shall be complete, so that it will be adequate for all times, because the novel conditions that constantly arise in the affairs of men, in laws and in deeds, are too numerous to count" (*Sefer HaIkarim*, discourse #3, chapter 23). We draw upon secular knowledge as we engage in holy endeavors. In an age of rapidly expanding information and understanding, to grasp fully human sexuality and its expressions, we believe it is necessary to gain insight and guidance from contemporary knowledge in related fields.

II. REFORM JEWISH SEXUAL VALUES

Jewish religious values are predicated upon the unity of God and the integrity of the world and its inhabitants as Divine creations. These values identify *Sh'leimut* as a fundamental goal of human experience. The Hebrew root *ShLM* expresses the ideal of wholeness, completeness, unity, and peace. Sexuality and sexual expression are integral and powerful elements in the potential wholeness of human beings. Our tradition commands us to sanctify the basic elements of the human being through values that express the Divine in every person and in every relationship. Each Jew should seek to conduct his/her sexual life in a manner that elicits the intrinsic holiness within the person and the relationship. Thus can *sh'leimut* be realized. The specific values that follow are contemporary interpretations of human *sh'leimut*:

(1) **B'tzelem Elohim** ("in the image of God"). This fundamental Jewish idea, articulated in Genesis 1:27, "And God created Adam in the Divine image. . . male and female. . ." is at the core of all Jewish values. *B'tzelem Elohim* underscores the inherent dignity of

every person, woman and man, with the equal honor and respect due to each individual's integrity and sexual identity. *B'tzelem Elohim* requires each of us to value one's self and one's sexual partner and to be sensitive to his/her needs. Thus do we affirm that consensuality and mutuality are among the values necessary to validate a sexual relationship as spiritual and ethical and therefore "in the image of God."

(2) *Emet* ("truth"). Authentic and ethical human relationships should be grounded in both truth and honesty. "These are the things you are to do: speak the truth to one another, render true and perfect justice in your gates" (Zechariah 8:16). People can only truly know each other and appreciate the Divine in all people when they come to each other openly and honestly. Both partners in an intimate relationship should strive to communicate lovingly. They should tell each other what gives them sexual pleasure and what does not, and should honestly share their love as well as the challenges that their relationship presents to them. However, honesty which is destructive of the relationship lacks the quality of *rachamim*, mercy. "Mercy and truth shall meet, justice and peace shall embrace" (Psalm 85:11). For that reason, intimate partners should be mindful that there may be moments when they are better served by not being totally candid with each other. In addition, falsehood which manipulates is sinful. Dating partners must not lie to each other in order to mislead the other into a sexual relationship. Neither partner should use the other as a sexual object. Finally, parents should learn how to teach their children both the facts and the consequences of sexual behavior, physically, emotionally, and spiritually. Parents should then use that teaching to help their children face the realities of the contemporary world.

(3) *B'riut* ("health"). Our tradition enjoins upon us the responsibility to rejoice in and to maximize our physical, emotional, and spiritual health. "Blessed is our Eternal God, Creator of the universe, who has made our bodies with wisdom, combining veins, arteries, and vital organs into a finely balanced network" (*Gates of Prayer* [1975], page 284). Reform Judaism encourages adults of all ages and physical and mental capabilities to develop expressions of their sexuality that are both responsible and joyful. The abuse of human sexuality can be destructive to our emotional, spiritual,

and physical health. We have a duty to engage only in those sexual behaviors that do not put others or ourselves at risk. In our age of HIV/AIDS and epidemic sexually transmitted diseases, irresponsible sexual behavior can put our lives and the lives of others at risk. We must act upon the knowledge that our sexual behavior is linked to our physical health.

(4) *Mishpat* ("justice"). Judaism enjoins upon us the mandate to reach out and care for others, to treat all of those created in the image of God with respect and dignity, to strive to create equality and justice wherever people are treated unfairly, to help meet the needs of the less fortunate, and to engage in *tikkun olam*, the repair of God's creation. The prophet Amos exhorts us to "let justice well up as waters, righteousness as a mighty stream" (Amos 5:24). As a people who have historically suffered at the hands of the powerful, we must be especially sensitive to any abuse of power and victimization of other human beings. According to the Sages, the *yetzer hara*, through its sexual component, may sometimes lead to destructive behavior and to sin. All forms of sexual harassment, incest, child molestation, and rape violate the value of *mishpat*. Our pursuit of *mishpat* should inspire us to eradicate prejudice, inequality, and discrimination based upon gender or sexual orientation.

(5) *Mishpachah* ("family"). The family is a cornerstone of Jewish life. The Torah, through the first mitzvah (Genesis 1:28), *p'ru ur'vu*, "be fruitful and multiply," emphasizes the obligation of bringing children into the world through the institution of the family. In our age, the traditional notion of family as being two parents and children (and perhaps older generations) living in the same household is in the process of being redefined. Men and women of various ages living together, singles, gay and lesbian couples, single-parent households, etc., may all be understood as families in the wider, if not traditional, sense. "Family" also has multiple meanings in an age of increasingly complex biotechnology and choice. While procreation and family are especially important as guarantors of the survival of the Jewish people, all Jews have a responsibility to raise and nurture the next generation of our people. The importance of family, whether biologically or

relationally based, remains the foundation of meaningful human existence.

(6) *Tz'niut* ("modesty"). The classic *Iggeret HaKodesh*, "The Holy Letter," sets forth the Jewish view that the Holy One did not create anything that is not beautiful and potentially good. The human body in itself is never to be considered an object of shame or embarrassment. Instead, ". . . it is the manner and context in which it [i.e., the body] is utilized, the ends to which it is used, which determine condemnation or praise." Our behavior should never reduce the human body to an object. Dress, language, and behavior should reflect a sensitivity to the Jewish respect for modesty and privacy. As Jews we acknowledge and celebrate the differences between public, private, and holy time as well as the differences between public, private, and holy places.

(7) *B'rit* ("covenantal relationship"). For sexual expression in human relationships to reach the fullness of its potential, it should be grounded in fidelity and the intention of permanence. This grounding mirrors the historic Jewish ideal of the relationship between God and the people Israel, with its mutual responsibilities and its assumption of constancy. The prophet Hosea wrote, "I will betroth you to Me forever; I will betroth you to Me in righteousness and justice, in love and compassion, I will betroth you to Me in everlasting faithfulness" (Hosea 2:21–22). A sexual relationship is covenantal when it is stable and enduring and includes mutual esteem, trust, and faithfulness.

(8) *Simchah* ("joy"). Human sexuality, as a powerful force in our lives, has the potential for physical closeness and pleasure, emotional intimacy and communication. The experience of sexual pleasure and orgasm, both in relationships and individually, can greatly delight women and men. Our tradition teaches that procreation is not the sole purpose of sexual intimacy; it not only recognizes but rejoices in the gratification which our sexuality can bring to us. As an expression of love, the physical release and relaxation, the enjoyment of sensuality and playfulness, which responsible sexual activity can provide is encouraged by our Jewish tradition. The Sages teach that the *Shechinah*, the Divine Presence, joins with people when they unite in love, but add that if there is no joy between them, the *Shechinah* will not be present

(*Shabbat* 30b, *Zohar* l). Judaism insists that the *simchah* of human sexual activity should be experienced only in healthy and responsible human relationships.

(9) **Ahavah** ("love"). The mitzvah from Leviticus 19:18, "You shall love your neighbor as yourself; I am *Adonai*," serves as an essential maxim of all human relationships. The same Hebrew value term, *ahavah*, is used to describe the ideal relationship between God and humanity as well as between people. The Jewish marriage ceremony speaks of "*ahavah v'achavah, shalom v'rei-ut*, "love and affection, wholeness and friendship" as ideals which should undergird holy relationships. For Jews *ahavah* is not only a feeling or emotion, but also the concrete behaviors we display toward God and our fellow humans. *Ahavah* implies "self esteem," the internal conviction that each of us should appear worthy in our own eyes. To be loved, one must consider oneself lovable; without regard for self, one can hardly care for others. *Ahavah* forbids any abuse or violence in sexual or any aspect of human relationships. *Ahavah* should be expressed through behavior which displays caring, support, and empathy.

(10) **K'dushah** ("holiness"). This value comes from the root meaning of the Hebrew word *KDSh*, "distinct from all others, unique, set apart for an elevated purpose." The Torah instructs us: "You shall be holy, for I, *Adonai* your God, am holy" (Leviticus 19:2). Holiness is not simply a state of being; rather it is a continuing process of human striving for increasingly higher levels of moral living. In a Reform Jewish context, a relationship may attain a measure of *k'dushah* when both partners voluntarily set themselves apart exclusively for each other, thereby finding unique emotional, sexual, and spiritual intimacy.

Our Torah teaches that, on the eve of Jacob's meeting and reconciliation with his brother Esau, he wrestled with a manifestation of Divinity and was wounded. The text continues: *v'yavo Yaakov shaleim*, "and Jacob arrived *shaleim*" following his struggles with himself and others. Thus did he become known as Yisrael, "the one who wrestles with God." We, too, as *B'nei/B'not Yisrael*, the spiritual descendants of Jacob, as human beings and as liberal Jews, wrestle with ourselves and our lives to achieve a measure of *sh'leimut*. May the Sexual Values described in this statement be for Reform Jews a source of guidance that leads us to a life of holiness.

While the committee was convened to examine a wide range of issues related to human sexuality, it has been called upon to focus first on gay and lesbian relationships. Our process began with an identification of values that characterize an ideal Jewish sexual relationship. We reviewed the traditional unique status of heterosexual, monogamous marriage in Judaism. And we studied gay and lesbian relationships in the context of the values contained in the above report.

III. CONCLUSIONS

At this moment in the history of the CCAR, the issue of rabbinic officiation at same-gender ceremonies is a matter of concern for many of our colleagues. These Reform Jewish Sexual Values have led the Ad Hoc Committee on Human Sexuality to conclude that *k'dushah* may be present in committed, same-gender relationships between two Jews, and that these relationships can serve as the foundation of stable Jewish families, thus adding strength to the Jewish community. In this spirit, we believe that the relationship of a Jewish, same-gender couple is worthy of affirmation through appropriate Jewish ritual, and that each rabbi should decide about officiation according to his/her own informed rabbinic conscience. We call upon the CCAR to support all colleagues in their choices in this matter. We also call upon the CCAR to develop educational programs in this area.

The Ad Hoc Committee on Human Sexuality considers this an interim report on the progress of its deliberations. We intend to continue exploring the dozens of issues involved in this important arena of human behavior and to bring additional guidance to our Movement on issues of human sexuality.

Further Reading and Resources

General

Dorff, Elliot N. *This is My Beloved, This Is My Friend: A Rabbinic Letter on Intimate Relations*. New York: The Rabbinical Assembly, 1996.

Einstein, Steve, and Lydia Kukoff. *Introduction to Judaism: A Source Book*. New York: UAHC Press, 1999.

Stern, Chaim. *On the Doorposts of Your House: Prayers and Ceremonies for the Jewish Home*. New York: CCAR Press, 1994.

Syme, Daniel. *The Jewish Home: A Guide for Jewish Living*. New York: UAHC Press, 1988.

Washofsky, Mark. *Jewish Living: A Guide to Contemporary Reform Practice*. New York: UAHC Press, 2001.

Wiener, Nancy H. *Beyond Breaking the Glass: A Spiritual Guide to Your Jewish Wedding*. New York: CCAR Press, 2001.

For Interfaith Couples

Cowan, Paul, and Rachel Cowan. *Mixed Blessings: Marriage Between Jews and Christians*. New York: Doubleday, 1987.

Glaser, Gabrielle. *Strangers to the Tribe*. New York: Houghton Mifflin, 1997.

King, Andrea. *If I'm Jewish and You're Christian, What are the Kids?* New York: UAHC Press, 1993.

Petsonk, Judy, and Remsen, Jim. *The Intermarriage Handbook: A Guide for Jews and Christians*. New York: William Morrow, 1988.

Schneider, Susan Weidman. *Intermarriage: The Challenge of Living with Differences Between Christains and Jews*, The Free Press, Macmillan Publishing Co., Inc., 1989.

The Union of American Hebrew Congregations also offers courses and workshops for interfaith couples, including:

Introduction to Judaism
Times and Seasons
Yours, Mine, and Ours

You can get information about these and other programs sponsored by the Reform Movement by contacting the central office: 212-650-4230.

For Gay and Lesbian Couples

Kahn, Yoel. *Kiddushin: Union Ceremonies for Lesbian and Gay Jews.* San Francisco: Congregation Sha'ar Zahav, 1994.

"The Kedushah of Homosexual Relationships." *CCAR Yearbook* 99 (1989) 136–145.

New Menorah Journal 59 (spring 5760/2000). "Same Sex Marriage in Our Generation."

This broad-based introduction includes the following articles:

"Learning about Homosexuality and Taking a New Stand" by Elliot N. Dorff

"Premarital Counseling" by Rabbi Nancy H. Wiener

"Legal Protections" by Susan Saxe

"Honor the Holiness of Lesbian and Gay Marriages" by Rabbi Sue Levi Elwell

"A Covenant of Same-Sex *Nisu'in* and *Kidushin*" by Eyal Levenson

"Gay Marriage—What's the Fuss" by Susan Saxe

"Same-Sex Marriage and the Law" by Rabbi Rebecca Alpert

"A 'Becoming' of a New Sexual Ethic" by Rabbi Arthur Waskow

Glossary

Avot D'Rabbi Natan	A collection of early rabbinic teachings on ethical behavior that were not included in the Mishnah. It was compiled in the second century C.E. by Rabbi Natan of Babylonia.
Baal Shem Tov	Literally, "Master of the Good Name," the popular nickname of the founder of Chasidism, Israel ben Eliezer. The Baal Shem Tov's emphasis on God's immanence revolutionized Jewish life and inspired a new movement of Judaism.
B'reishit Rabbah	A collection of midrash compiled in the fifth century C.E., which offers explanations and meanings for the stories found in Genesis.
C.E.	Abbreviation for Common Era. This term, while recognizing that throughout the world the year "0," defined by Christians as the year of Jesus' birth, ushered in a new era, does not mention Jesus. Many scholars, Jewish and non-Jewish, choose to use C.E. (Common Era) and B.C.E. (before the Common Era), rather than the specifically Christian B.C. (before Christ) and A.D. (*anno Domini* [in the Year of our Lord (Jesus)]).
Eliyahu Rabbah	The major part of a midrashic work known as *Seder Eliyahu* or *Tanna D'Vei Eliyahu*. Scholars disagree as to the work's authorship and place of origin, but there is some agreement that the midrash was written down in the seventh century C.E. The midrash is divided into two parts: *Seder Eliyahu Rabbah* (The Major Order of Eliyahu) and *Seder Eliyahu Zuta* (The Minor Order of Eliyahu).
Sh'mot Rabbah	A compilation of midrashim on the Book of Exodus written down in the tenth or eleventh century but containing earlier materials.

Gates of Prayer	A prayer book for daily, Sabbath, and holiday worship, published by the Reform Movement. Originally released in 1976, it has gone through a number of revisions, to reflect greater gender sensitivity.
Iggeret HaKodesh	"The Holy Letter" is a medieval philosophic and mystical treatise on marital relations and behavior. Its authorship is unknown.
Likutei Moharan	A work by the Chasidic master Nachman of Bratzlav published in 1806. Nachman's first published work, it includes theology and biblical interpretation.
Midrash	From the Hebrew verb lidrosh, to "seek out," midrash is a form of literature that seeks out meanings from biblical texts. Through reflection, explanation, and story, midrash offers readers of different generations ways to relate to and find meaning for their own lives in the Bible.
Midrash Rabbah	A tenth-century compilation of rabbinic stories and explanations, midrash, on the many books of the Bible.
Midrash T'hillim	A tenth- or eleventh-century compilation of midrash on the Book of Psalms (in Hebrew, *T'hillim*).
Mishnah	The first compilation of rabbinic discussions about the meaning and application of Torah laws for the lives of later generations. Known as the Oral Torah, it was edited by Rabbi Y'hudah HaNasi in 200 C.E.
Pirkei Avot	A portion of the Mishnah focusing on the ethical teachings of the Rabbis.
Pirkei D'Rabbi Eliezer	This collection of midrash on Genesis and the first chapters of Exodus is named Eliezer ben Hyrcanus, the first-century-C.E. Rabbi who is credited with its authorship.
Shulchan Aruch	Literally, "The Prepared Table." A code of Jewish law attributed to Joseph Karo in 1565 C.E., which became authoritative for Judaism.
Talmud	Following the editing of the Mishnah, the Rabbis continued to discuss the meaning and application of Torah laws for their generations. The Rabbis of the two largest Jewish communities, Babylonia and Jerusalem, compiled their discussions and decisions (from approximately the second to the fifth centuries) and completed the work of the Mishnah. The Hebrew verb for finish is *gamar*; the works of these Rabbis was known as Gemara. The Mishnah and Gemara of these two communities are known as Talmuds (in Hebrew, "teach-

ings"). Jews still study the teachings of the Babylonian and Jerusalem Talmuds. In Hebrew they are known as the Talmud Bavli and the *Talmud Y'rushalmi*.

Tobit	Part of the Apocrypha, writings considered sacred but not included in the *Tanach* (The Jewish canon). Tobit is part of the Christian canon.
Tosefta	This third-century-C.E. collection of rabbinic teachings contains material not found in the Mishnah, but produced by the same generations of Rabbis. Rabbi Chiya and his disciples have been credited with editing this work.
Zohar	A thirteenth-century Jewish mystical classic, known in English as "The Book of Splendor." The *Zohar* was written by Moses de Leon but was pseudoepigraphically attributed to Shimon bar Yochai.
Zohar Chadash	The fifth section of the *Zohar*. Abraham ben Eliezer HaLevi B'ruchim edited this mystical text and adjoined it to the other sections of the *Zohar*, forming the central work of Jewish mysticism.